C000214554

The Remarkable Trees of St Albans

To Doug & Pat

Best wishes

Kate Bretherton

and Donato Cinicolo
11/05/2011

by

Kate Bretherton

KATE BRETHERTON
Flint Barn, Norrington End, Redding Lane, Redbourn, AL3 7QN;
kate@walk-talk.co.uk; www.walk-talk.co.uk

Information on this title: as above or info@walk-talk.co.uk

© Kate Bretherton 2010

Published by Kate Bretherton

This publication is in copyright. Subject to statutory exception and to the provisions
of relevant collective licensing agreements, no replication of any part may take place
without the written permission of Kate Bretherton.

First published 2010

Typeset by Flower Typesetting (enquire@flowertypesetting.co.uk)

Printed through SS Media Limited: 88 Sandy Lane South, Wallington,
Surrey, SM6 9 RQ; info@ss-media.co.uk; www.ss-media.co.uk.

A catalogue record for this publication is available from the British Library

ISBN 978-0-9567399-0-2

The publisher accepts no responsibility for the persistence or accuracy of URLs for
external or third-party Internet websites referred to in this publication, and does not
guarantee that any content on such websites is, or will remain, accurate or appropriate.

Front cover illustration: Willow tree at St Michaels ford.

Back cover illustration: Bark of the sycamore tree in the open space where
Waverley Road joins Batchwood Drive.

Contents

Foreword   v

Preface   vii

Acknowledgements   vii

Paul Arnold's trees planted for their historical connections   2

Trees with history   34

Our favourite trees   48

St Albans city parks   122

St Albans churchyards   160

Batchwood   170

Harpenden and Rothamsted   187

Villages, woodlands and the countryside   195

Street trees and garden trees   217

Tree management   225

Trees and the future   235

References   241

Foreword

Trees are one of the most important natural elements within the urban landscape of the City and District of St Albans. Whether appearing individually, in groups or as woodlands, trees are essential to life and their value cannot be overstated. They:

- are an important part of the landscape and contribute to people's quality of life and sense of well being;
- release oxygen for us to breathe;
- absorb carbon dioxide (thereby reducing the greenhouse effect);
- filter air and reduce other pollutants such as ozone, nitrogen oxides, sulphur dioxides, carbon monoxide, smoke, dust and ash;
- increase biodiversity by providing a variety of habitats for wildlife – a mature tree can provide support for over 460 different mammals, birds and insects;
- provide a renewable resource of timber, fruit, seeds, nuts and fuel;
- create aesthetic value, improving the appearance of our environment by providing a variety of scale, form, colour and shape;
- reduce wind speeds, giving shelter and comfort;
- reduce noise levels;
- reduce flash flooding;
- reduce everyday stress, particularly important in today's environment – research has shown that hospital patients recover more quickly when able to enjoy the view of trees;
- provide shade from the sun and make areas more attractive to live and work in;
- positively affect property values and help to attract investment.

Opposite: An ancient beech in the abbey churchyard right in the heart of town reminds us of how much less our lives would be without trees

David Curry
October 2010

Preface

Are the trees in this book remarkable?

Some are remarkable in the way in which we would expect: they are old or rare or of exceptional beauty.

Many trees have none of these characteristics but someone in our community finds them remarkable for their associations – the memories or ideas that the tree evokes. Where people have been willing to share these associations with us, their trees have been included and I hope you will enjoy their stories as much as I have done.

I would also say that St Albans District's trees as a whole are remarkable: we are rich in specimen trees, in native woodlands, trees in streets, parks and churchyards.

Photographs can sometimes change our perception and, if anyone's photographs can do that, Donato Cinicolo's can. Then, having seen the photograph, or heard of an interesting association, there is the different experience of seeing the tree for oneself, being near the tree, being under its branches. I hope this book will lead you to new awareness, new experiences and an increased enjoyment of the wonderful trees around us.

Acknowledgements

This book was produced under the auspices of St Albans District Council Tree Warden Scheme. My thanks go to David Curry, Co-ordinator of the Tree Warden Scheme for his steady mentoring through the whole challenging process; to all those people who told us of their favourite trees – or trees that needed to be included in a book about St Albans trees; to Donato Cinicolo for his wonderful photographs – and for making our expeditions to find the trees such enjoyable adventures; to Anne Valentine for convincing me that, to do a proper job, I needed professional page layout and proof reading; to Jane Flower of Flower Typesetting for setting out the pages so attractively and coping with all the implications of my being a novice author and publisher; to Chris Pudsey for doing a combined editing and proof-reading job to a tight deadline; and to my friends for their tolerance and support while I have been obsessed with the book.

Kate Bretherton
October 2010

Opposite:
Sander's Mexican lime in Camp Road is a remarkable tree in every way: it is rare, ancient, magnificent, beautiful and has an interesting history

Paul Arnold's trees planted for their historical connections

When Paul Arnold told me about the trees he had planted for their historical connections, I wanted everyone interested in St Albans now and in the future to know about them – and that is how this book came to be written.

The project has widened to include trees in our parks and streets, people's specific favourites and some issues to do with trees, but it is Paul's trees and how they came to be planted that has been my inspiration.

Paul had been a forester in Lincolnshire and in Hertfordshire and came to work for St Albans City Parks Department in the 1970s. Once it occurred to him to plant trees for their historical connections, he came up with all sorts of ideas. The trees that resulted are a life-enhancing legacy for us all.

This opening chapter is what Paul Arnold told me about his trees.

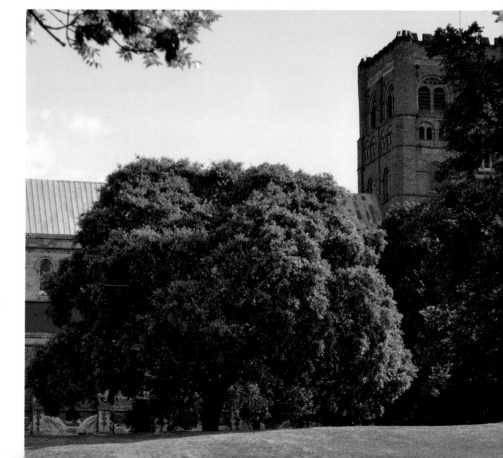

Opposite: Paul
Arnold in 2010

Right: Paul's
ecumenical
holm oak

The French Connection

Paul Arnold's project of planting trees for their historical connections started when the St Albans Civic Society was concerned about 'the dreadful state' of the area where the drinking fountain used to be between the Clock Tower and the High Street at the end of French Row.

Council departments, Paul tells us, were often under fire from the Civic Society so he thought it was astute of Mr Plant, Head of the Parks Department at the time, to suggest to them that they design the layout and the Parks Department would put it into effect. This turned out to be a good idea because even within the Society there was considerable disagreement and the Parks people were glad to be out of the politics.

The layout included a circle of benches and shaped paving stones to represent three circular landmarks that had been on this site: the 13th century Eleanor Cross, the 18th century Market Cross and water pump, and the 19th century drinking fountain. The layout also included a tree.

Initially, the tree was to be positioned close to the Great Red Lion (now Zizzi's) – too close for the Parks Department because, by then, the effects of trees on building subsidence was beginning to be understood. The Civic Society agreed to a new position a little further from the buildings.

What sort of tree should they plant? The adjacent French Row made Paul Arnold think of the famous French gardener Jean Robin and the tree named after him, the robinia. Paul had made his first historical connection.

It is in Jean Robin's gardens at the French Court of Henry IV and Louis XIII that the tree is first known in Europe, and it was through Robin's friendship and collaboration with John Tradescant the Elder that the robinia was introduced to this country. John Tradescant was employed by the Cecil family at Theobald Palace and then at nearby Hatfield House. The jaunty image of a gardener in knee-length puffed-out trousers and tall hat carved into the great staircase of the house is thought to be a portrait of John Tradescant the Elder.

The robinia has light and airy leaves and lovely upward-reaching, zig-zagging branches.

The bark is deeply grooved and, with age, becomes gnarled and interestingly weird.

The flowers are white and clustered in cascades. I saw a young woman cup a cascade in her two hands and draw it against her cheek. It was a precious moment.

Robinia flowers

A single robinia flower

Do the flowers remind you of sweet pea or runner bean flowers? They are all in the same family and used to be called Leguminosae but are now Fabaciae.

The robinia is a native of North America and its common names are false acacia, locust tree and black locust. Mimosa trees, which grow in Australia and Africa, are real acacias. They have more feathery leaves than the robinia but are also Fabaciae.

But why do you think the robinia is called a locust tree? The story is stranger than fiction.

At the end of French Row we have a robinia planted for its French connection

Early Pilgrim Fathers knew the Bible story of John the Baptist being sustained by locusts when he dwelt in the wilderness, but they also thought that it was not really insects but carob pods that he ate, so, when they saw a tree with what looked like carob pods, they called it a locust tree. What is truly brilliant

A robinia pod

fun is that there is no ambiguity about the original Hebrew word used, and scholars now accept that the Gospels tell us that St John ate locust insects. The current Greek word for locust, *akris*, was sometimes used in the ancient world to mean carob, which is presumably the origin of the confusion, but my guess is that it caught on because squeamish Westerners did not like the idea of their saint doing anything as primitive as eating insects.

Unfortunately the robinia pods have nothing like the chocolate-flavoured sticky pulp found round carob seeds.

And what of French Row and its French connection? A shiny black board outside The Fleur de Lys tells us that John, King of France, when he was captured after the Battle of Poitiers in 1356, was held in a building on this site. However, the illustrated board at the entrance to the side passage casts doubt on King John of France ever having been held here in French Row.

Rather than King John of France staying here, it might have been a group of French mercenaries recruited by the barons more than a century earlier in 1216 to help curb our own bad King John.

There is certainly a tradition of a French connection here – the name of the passage commemorates it – and it is right that a tree should do the same.

Information on a board close by casts doubt on King John of France having been held in French Row

Verdun: the last tree left standing

The St Albans City Parks Department started to purchase trees in containers and their supplier was a nursery in Surrey. The nurseryman there had been over to France to the battlefields of Verdun and he brought back some conkers from the only tree left standing after the battle.

When Paul Arnold, on a trip to the nursery, heard the story he asked for one of the seedlings. The nurseryman had a habit of planting seeds in obsolete metal milk crates and that is probably where our conker started its life. A City Guide told me that she had often wondered why the Battle of Verdun, very much a French-German battle, had been chosen to be commemorated. Can we call Paul Arnold's encounter with the Surrey nurseryman a lucky chance?

On his return, Paul selected a place for the sapling in Waxhouse Gate and contacted the British Legion in St Albans. There was one surviving 'Old Contemptible' among their membership and it was he who planted the tree on the anniversary of Verdun to commemorate the battle and in memory of the men who lost their lives.

'Old Contemptible' was the title proudly adopted by the men of the British Expeditionary Force who saw service before or on 22nd November 1914. They derive their title from the famous Order of the Day given by Kaiser Wilhelm II on 19 August 1914 '... to walk over General French's contemptible little Army'. This is obviously a translation, but the irony of the derogatory term is inescapable: these were brave and tenacious men, the first of an army that was – eventually and after tragic losses – victorious.

A sombre occasion to commemorate all those lost at the Battle of Verdun

For many decades, all survivors of the First World War were honoured with the title, but by the time we were down to only a very few survivors, we seemed no longer willing to use the term, even in conscious irony.

I pictured the Battle of Verdun being fought across a field and lasting for some days. The battle took place over more than 60 square miles; fierce bombardment and hand-to-hand fighting lasted for 10 months and skirmishes continued for another 2 years.

The opening attack on 21 February 1916 was from a barrage of 1,400 guns ranged over 8 miles.

The equivalent, if St Albans were the objective, would be fire from a line of 1,400 guns – mortars – from Harpenden to Welwyn Garden City trained on our defences dotted around the villages in between, smashing through homes, pubs, churches, woodlands, into hillsides, sending mud flying everywhere and creating a quagmire and heaps of rubble and timber.

The town of Verdun has a citadel within it and to the north east of the town and east of the River Meuse there was a network of 18 forts with passages below ground and turrets with rotating artillery above but, by 1916, a good deal of the artillery had been taken from Verdun forts to be used elsewhere leaving the area vulnerable.

Maps of the battle show wiggling lines of the German advance towards Verdun with labels '24 Feb', '9 April', '8 Aug'. Fort after fort was taken, many of them hard won with fighting day after day, barricade by barricade, sometimes in narrow underground corridors.

Both sides suffered terribly. *'Ils ne passerout pas!'* was General Robert Nivelle's official order of the day on 23 June 1916. The expression has become a byword for French resolve, and Verdun a byword for French tenacity.

So, of what relevance is this tragic battle to Britain and St Albans?

The French defense of Verdun meant that the Kaiser had depleted resources to withstand the Russian attack on his Eastern Front in the late summer of 1916.

Verdun meant that the Kaiser did not reach Paris. Nor win the war.

Our Verdun horsechestnut is tall and beautiful

In late March, from each sticky bud formed the previous autumn, comes leaf after leaf, a flower bud, and more leaves, each leaf large and palmate. It is like a magician producing strings of silk handkerchiefs out of a hat – only here the hat is as small as the top of my finger and the handkerchiefs bigger than my hands. The leaves are cream-coloured and furry at first, swelling into a wholesome green palmate shape of up to seven leaflets.

Opposite: The horsechestnut planted for the Battle of Verdun

Masses of flowers open soon after the leaves. They appear in clusters, panicles, that look like candles. Each panicle is made up of up to 40 pink-spotted, five-petalled flowers.

Then the tree seems to relax into its own spreading beauty for the summer, the insect-pollinated flowers mutating into mahogany-glossy conkers, each in its round spiny green case.

Horsechestnut flower

In autumn, each leaf takes on more than one colour: shades of reds and browns and oranges and vestigial greens. And, long before the leaves are ready to drop, the distinctive sticky buds that hold next year's leaves and flowers begin to appear.

There is another reason that a horse-chestnut is an appropriate tree to represent a battle. In both

Verdun horsechestnut in bloom

world wars, the starch from conkers was used to produce acetone required to gelatinise the mixture of guncotton, nitroglycerine and petroleum jelly that makes up cordite, an almost smokeless explosive. Crown Prince Willem, on that first day alone of the battle, fired 100,000 shells an hour for 21 hours into the French defences. The fact that cordite emits no more than a blue haze when fired makes it score over gunpowder, the smoke from which can obscure a gunner's view – or give away the position of a sniper.

A more positive use of the horsechestnut fruits is as soap. When mixed with cold soft water, the saponins found within conkers make a lather which is an effective soap. Try it with the leaves, which also have saponins: get someone to pour a little water over a horsechestnut leaf in your hands and rub vigorously until a slippery lather develops that leaves your hands soft and clean.

Soapwort is even richer in saponins and is used in the cleaning of the Bayeaux Tapestry.

A golden ash for justice

It was Penny Jones who suggested planting, on behalf of Amnesty International St Albans group, a tree to commemorate 'The Year of the Prisoner of Conscience' in 1976. She asked Paul Arnold to advise on a suitable tree and he chose an ash tree because of the Saxon tradition that justice should be dispensed under an ash tree.

Paul went with Penny Jones to Ayletts Nursery to make sure that the tree was a good one. They chose a fine specimen of a golden-leafed ash, *Faximus transioni*. The Parks Department dug the hole for the tree and supervised its planting in the top corner of Vintry Gardens, the corner diagonally opposite the Abbey.

Amnesty International head office supported the scheme and suggested that Mukhtar Rana, who had been a prisoner of conscience for 20 years in Pakistan, should be involved in planting the tree and speaking on behalf of prisoners of conscience and the way in which Amnesty International had helped in keeping his plight from being forgotten.

The tree was planted in a formal ceremony and Mukhtar Rana, a charismatic speaker, did the occasion justice. After his release, Mukhtar Rana was chairman of Peace and Human Rights Trust International and campaigned tirelessly and effectively for human rights.

Female ash flowers

Ash leaf buds are one of the few I can recognise in winter. They are right at the tip of the twig and as black as nature can get them and as steeply conical as an ancient Assyrian's pointed iron helmet. Beneath and on either side of

Olive flower

the leaf bud are found the smaller but also sooty and conical flower buds. The flowers come out before the leaves – which makes the ash a 'precocious' tree. At first the flower buds swell into a tight tiny fist of purple balls and then these elongate on creamy green stalks, the male flowers opening yellow with slender anthers, the female flowers opening more widely into a filigree of purple and then pale green – a bit like cream-stalked, purple-headed broccoli florets.

The ash is sexually confused – or perhaps we should say the species is 'sexually all-encompassing': some trees have all male flowers, and some have all female flowers, some have a single branch or two of one sex and all other branches of the other sex, some are male one year and female the next, and some trees have hermaphrodite flowers (each with both male and female parts). I like it that the botanical term for such hermaphrodite flowers is 'perfect'. The definition confirms what we all knew: humans are not perfect.

Fertilised flowers with female parts produce bunches of dry seeds known as 'keys', and these tend to hang on the tree right through winter, making the ash distinctive.

Our common name for the ash is the Saxon word for it: aesc, which also meant 'spear'. Its wood is pale, light and flexible making it ideal for tool handles, baseball bats, oars and, when steamed and bent, for bentwood furniture, umbrella handles and the like. The ash is a tree with practical uses.

Ash trees belong to the same family as olives, the Oleaceae, which is, to me, unexpected because their flowers and fruits, on which the taxonomy is usually based, seem so dissimilar. Can you see any similarity in the flowers? Or between ash keys and olives? But who are we to know: taxonomists have been working hard on the order Lamiales and they seem to have no doubt that the ash, olive, privet, forsythia, lilac and jasmine spring from a common ancestor, distinct from the ancestors of other families in the same order (Tudge, 2006).

I had difficulty in substantiating the tradition that the Saxons associated ash trees with justice. I searched the Saxon Chronicles (now online) to no avail. That was only negative information, however, not evidence that moots were or were not held under ash trees. I asked at the Museum of St Albans but was told that moots were held in important places, Maiden Castle, for example, but not, as far as they knew, particularly under ash trees. I was told that the Saxons did regard the ash as a significant tree: Edward the Confessor's Charter granting the Manor of Wheathamstead to Westminster Abbey defined its boundaries by the location of ash trees.

Paul Arnold's source for the tradition was '*Trees of the British Isles in history and legend*' (Wilks, 1972). Wilks tells us that it was the gods in Teutonic legend who held court (was it even a court of justice?) under a mythical ash tree, the World Tree, Yggdrasil, that reached to heaven and had roots down to the 'infernal regions' with squirrels reporting what was going on amongst the gods to an eagle in the topmost branches.

An intriguing legend, but it is not an association worthy of Amnesty International's valiant fight for justice.

Opposite: The golden ash planted for justice

I was then told by Chris Saunders, who used to work at the Museum, that in our own St Albans, the Abbot held his manorial court under the Great Ash in the Abbey courtyard. He directed me to the Victoria History of Hertfordshire which is online, and there we can read that 'For the trial of all crimes, pleas, and plaints the townspeople had to go to the Hundred Court of the Abbot's Liberty, which was held before the steward of the liberty under the great ash tree in the courtyard of the abbey.' Equivalent courts were held under ash trees in Midhurst (in what is now West Sussex) and Swathling (now a suburb of Southampton).

Imperfect as the hundred courts were, at least we can be sure of the link between ash trees and earthly courts of would-be justice.

Holm oak for ecumenism

There was a surge of support for the ecumenical movement in the 1970s and Paul Arnold wanted to do what he could to support it. He had read in J. H. Wilks' 'Trees of the British Isles in history and legend' that, for people in Tudor times, holm oaks symbolised the Papacy and that many were destroyed by Protestants in the purges of 1536 (Wilks, p115). I can find no corroboration of Wilks' statements but no evidence found is not proof that it did not happen, and we have as near as we can get to a tree that represents Roman Catholicism. Paul thought it would be a good ecumenical gesture to plant the Catholic tree in the grounds of the Protestant cathedral: the tree could commemorate the only English pope, Nicholas Breakspear who became Pope Adrian IV.

The authorities at the cathedral accepted Paul Arnold's suggestion and the local Roman Catholic community was keen and sent word to Rome; and the pope was pleased to send an apostolic delegate to officially plant the tree.

The holm oak destined for the Abbey Orchard was in the Council nurseries in New Greens. It was a big tree and hard work to move. The team dug trenches on four sides of the tree and lowered a steel hawser into the trenches. They dug a trench from the trenches to a nearby telegraph pole and anchored the hawser to it. They then tightened the hawser until it sliced like cheese wire through the huge root ball of the tree. They encased the tree and its roots and surrounding earth in sacking, 'like a pudding cloth', and used a skip lorry to transport it through the streets of St Albans before the crack of dawn, careful all the way to avoid telegraph wires. The skip lorry was a brilliant transporter because it was low slung and had the mechanism to swing the tree outwards.

A hole of appropriate enormous size was dug, not without difficulty. As they dug, the men came upon the top of a brick arch. A member of the Museum

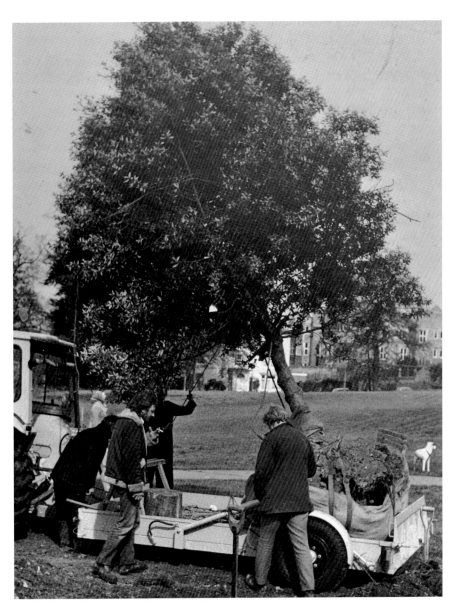

The holm oak
arriving on a skip
lorry

staff had to be consulted and he suggested it was the top of a tunnel from the Abbey to the Sopwell nunnery. He was joking – there are always stories of underground tunnels from monasteries to nunneries, but I understand that they are not generally given credence and certainly not here. There are, however, tunnels from the Abbey towards George Street perhaps for ease of provisioning, and there are remarkably substantial underground drains that lead from the Abbey roof gutters down into Abbey Orchard. The drains are

The skip lorry
swung the holm
oak into position

big enough for men to crawl through and it was probably one of these that the
Parks people encountered.

Another hole was dug clear of the arch and the tree lowered into the hole,
the arms of the skip lorry swinging it out and down into the hole.

The men packed a good bit of soil round the tree but left some space
and more of the compost made from autumn leaf sweepings to finish the
job. They also left a small heap of carefully sifted compost for the official
'planting'. When it is a lady mayor doing the job, a spoonful of soil is put on
a dainty trowel, the trowel is held while photographs are taken and then the
trowel is tipped to let the soil trickle round the base of the tree while more
photographs are taken. However, the apostolic delegate was no lady mayor but
of the more robust Christian kind and knew how to shovel soil and plant a
tree properly. He polished off the sifted compost in one sweep and then dug
his shovel into the unsifted compost.

'We are going to get the last laugh,' said one of the Parks men. They had
not been included in the introductions to the apostolic delegate: the cathedral

Opposite: The
holm oak planted
for ecumenism

THE REMARKABLE TREES OF ST ALBANS

officers at the time had presented him to the civic dignitaries, the Lord High Sheriff of Hertfordshire and august churchmen, but not the Parks men. I can imagine how it was: the churchman would have had his head full of all sorts of responsibilities and names to remember and was distracted. However, the Parks people regarded the project as their own, and they were miffed.

The 'laugh' was that the composted leaves collected from pavements and park corners held all sorts of unexpected debris including condoms. It all floated into the air as the apostolic delegate shovelled the compost round the tree base. The latter, by the way, shook hands warmly with the Parks people when the planting was over.

There was a photograph of the planting in 'abbeynews' of 3 May 1974. The caption reads '... The apostolic delegate said at the ceremony ... that he hoped the ecumenical movement would deepen understanding between the Churches as the roots of the tree went deep into the soil, and that friendships between Churches would multiply like the leaves on its branches.' Our Abbey Orchard holm oak is densely leaved all year round and its roots must be deep in the soil to keep it growing so healthily. It is as if the tree is doing its part to encourage us to fulfil the apostolic delegate's plea for friendship between the churches.

To find the tree, walk down hill across the front of the west face of the cathedral, out through the railings into the Abbey Orchard and continue on the path ahead; you soon come to a four-way crossing of asphalt paths and the holm oak planted for ecumenism is right there.

The tree also commemorates Nicholas Breakspear whose family lived in Bedmond. His father, Robert, became a monk at St Albans Abbey. Accounts differ as to whether Nicholas was a pupil at the Abbey but he certainly was not accepted there as a monk. He went to France and became a lay brother, then ordained priest, prior and eventually abbot in the Augustinian monastery of St Rufus near Avignon. From there, he was called to Rome where he was consecrated Bishop of Albano, an area in the Alban hills south of Rome, and then created Cardinal.

In 1152, Eugenius III sent Cardinal Breakspear as Papal Legate to Scandinavia to help decide the organisation of the Church within Norway, Sweden and Denmark. It is perhaps significant that he was away for these two years. Sometimes, someone who has been away is not seen as belonging to the inevitable factions that develop within an institution, and is acceptable to all parties. This may have been the case, or it may have been that he was known for being 'prudent, scholarly and disciplined'. For whatever reasons, when Breakspear returned in 1154, he was elected pope and reigned as Adrian IV for four years.

It astonishes me that near-on a thousand years ago, a lad from Bedmond in Hertfordshire could establish himself in France and then Italy and travel to Scandinavia and back. I understand that he was moving within the institutions of the Church in which Latin was universally understood, and that latterly he had the protection and resources of the Church but, none the less, he covered thousands of miles across territories of many different languages.

The Holm oak, *Quercus ilex*, is also known as the holly oak: 'holm' is thought to be the Saxon word for holly. It is also widely known in Britain as the evergreen oak, despite not being the only oak that is evergreen: the cork oak (*Quercus suber*), live oak (*Quercus agrifolia*) and several others are, too.

Holm oak catkins and flowers in late May

Holm oak leaves are a glossy dark green on top and silvery beige and hairy underneath – and there are masses of them giving the tree a density throughout the year. The branches grow out and up so that the tree as a whole has a pleasing rounded shape.

Male catkins appear in early summer along with tiny pink-tipped female flowers. Acorns are smaller than those of the English oak, a vibrant green nestling deep in a plump grey textured cup.

On a guided walk round Kew gardens, we were told that oaks are particularly promiscuous trees leading to there being 300–600 species (depending who is counting) in the genus. To put this in context, there are only 10 species of chestnut and 10 species of beech, both genera being within the same family as the oak, the Fagaceae.

Hybridisation makes it hard for taxonomists to agree on where one species begins and another ends. There is also disagreement on which features reveal true evolutionary relationships, on which taxonomy aspires to be based. Holm oaks, in particular, do not fit comfortably into any of the genus-splitting now in progress (Tudge, 2005). Watch this space.

Stone pine for an ancient goddess

Visiting Verulamium Museum, Paul Arnold noticed on display a votive bowl filled with pine nuts because pine nuts, seeds of the stone pine, *Pinus pinea*, were found in excavations of the triangular temple in Roman Verulamium. Paul thought, 'That's our next historical tree planting'.

Paul Arnold knew from W. J. Bean's '*Trees and Shrubs Hardy in the British Isles*' that the 'tree [*Pinus pinea*] has always been valued in Italy for its edible seeds and, as their husks have been found in the refuse heaps of Roman encampments in Britain, they appear to have been sent over for the use of the army in occupation' (Bean 1980).

On hearing of this, I inferred, with my 21st century layman's understanding of offerings, that even a staple food such as was issued to soldiers would be an appropriate offering if presented in the right spirit to a god or goddess. However, Rosalind Niblett sheds a very different light on the *Pinus pinea* seeds:

> The suggestion that the temple was dedicated to Cybele is based on the discovery in what must have been votive pits in the temple court, of burnt seeds and scales from pine cones of the Italian pine (*Pinus pinea*). The pine figured in the rituals associated with the worship of Cybele and her consort Attis but the Italian pine is not a species that grows naturally in Britain, either the cones or a tree itself must have been imported.
>
> Niblett, 2001

Cybele was a goddess of earth, mountains and caverns and was worshipped as a protector of fortified places and cities in general. As great protectoress of cities, it is appropriate that her temple would be seen straight ahead through a triumphal arch as people entered Verulamium through the Londinium Gate. The temple had an external altar at its blunt point facing Londinium Gate with a backdrop of the plastered walls of the temple, probably embellished with Purbeck marble, fragments of which were found in the 1930s excavation (Niblett, 2001).

The cult of Cybele and her consort Attis increased in popularity in Britain through to the 4th century. For more about the bizarre rituals associated with Cybele and her priests, not recommended to be read too soon after breakfast, you could Google 'Catterick Attis'. Closer to home, 'An inscription on a pot found in a grave at Dunstable, 10 miles along Watling Street, tells us that the jar was dedicated to the dead person by a man called Regillinus, on behalf of fellow worshippers of Cybele' (Niblett, 2000). There is an informative display in Verulamium Museum about the temple, Cybele and her acolytes, who were called *dendrophori*.

Opposite: The stone pines planted for Cybele

The grove of *Pinus pinea* that Paul and the Parks people planted is as close to the triangular temple in Verulamium Park as the archaeological authorities would allow. Looking up the hill to the hypocaust building we see a line of trees going away to the left of it. It is towards the end of this line of trees that the grove was planted.

From plans of Verulamium that show the features in the Park, we can work out that the triangular temple is 50 metres from the concrete path along the hedge line lower down the hill and 200 metres from Londinium Gate. From the grove, Londinium Gate can be located by the red dog-poo box in front of its railings. A football pitch is about 90 metres long and there are usually a couple of pitches marked out and their goal posts clearly visible between the grove and Londinium Gate so that we can think 'two football pitches from the Gate and half a football pitch from the hedge'.

Not all the trees planted in the grove survived. Another name for the stone pine is 'umbrella pine' and this makes it easy for us to tell which are the original trees: they are distinctly rounded on top. When Paul Arnold saw that replacements were of different species of pine, he realised that the people now responsible for trees in St Albans do not know of the historical connections. It was Paul telling me this that made me determined that the stories behind the trees should not be quite lost.

American trees for Rotary beginnings

People in the Rotary Club of St Albans approached Paul Arnold with their idea to plant a circle of American trees to commemorate the anniversary of the founding of Rotary International in America. Paul advised on the species to be planted and Rotary sourced and supervised the planting in the top corner of Westminster Lodge parkland between the athletics track and Verulamium Park.

There is an English oak in the centre of the circle and, on a plinth topped by a circle of wood, is a silver plaque with the Rotary emblem flanked by the dates 1905 and 1980. It reads:

> The trees surrounding this English oak which are all of American origin were presented by the Rotary Club of St Albans Verulamium in the City of St Albans to commemorate the 75th anniversary of the founding of Rotary International in Chicago U.S.A. on 23rd February 1905.

The planned trees in the circle were American, but life is not always easy and we have long ago lost a pin oak, a red oak, a balm of Gilead, an Indian bean tree, a cotton wood and a white ash.

Opposite: The silver maple in the circle of American trees planted for Rotary beginnings

The trees we have now are interesting enough. If we take the plaque as the clock centre and 12 o'clock at the top of the hill, the trees are as follows:

At 6 o'clock, lowest down the hill, is a **silver maple**, *Acer saccharium*, not to be confused with *Acer saccharum*, the sugar maple. It is the tree that we first

see as we approach the circle from below, a large tree with branches arching upwards. It is a native of eastern North America. It has an obviously maple leaf, although particularly deeply incised and fluttering to show the paler underside from which it gets its common name. The flowers start to come out while the pointed

Silver maple leaves

leaf buds are still tight closed: the silver maple, like the ash, is precocious.

At 4 o'clock is a **box elder** or ash-leafed maple, *Acer negundo*, which has a most un-maple-like leaf. Most of the leaves are pinnate with 3, 5 or 7 leaflets but some of the leaflets are fused into a more maple-like three-lobed form: it is hard to believe they are leaves on the same tree. The flowers, too, are un-maple-like. Our tree is male and what we see in spring are clusters of long drooping

Box elder leaves

coral-coloured stamens. One of the distinguishing characteristics of the box elder is its smooth bright-green shoots, and it has an exciting twist to its bark. The box elder is distributed across eastern North America from Florida to Ontario. It came over here first in 1688 to the gardens of Bishop Henry Compton at Fulham Palace.

Box elder bark

Cockspur thorn leaves and flowers in spring

At 3 o'clock and 9 o'clock are **cockspur thorn** which is native to Eastern North America and is of the hawthorn family (*Crataegus*), species *crus-galli*. The leaves look nothing like the leaves of our ubiquitous common hawthorn, either in shape or texture. The flowers are white and prettily clustered in amongst the glossy bright green leaves which turn wonderful colours in autumn: purple browns and yellows, startling alongside brilliant crimson fruits. All cockspur thorn trees seem to grow at an angle like the ones in the circle.

Cockspur thorn leaves and flowers in autumn

Norway maple leaves

At 2 o'clock is a **Norway maple**, *Acer platanoides*, which is a native of Norway and not on the original plan but an attractive tree whose deep red petioles and purple-green foliage adds contrast during the summer.

At 12 o'clock on the outer circle and 9 o'clock on the inner circle are two substantial **American limes**, *Tilia americana*, the leaves of which are distinctively as dark a green above as below and as large as my large hand. I am told by woodworking friends that when they order lime wood from America they have to call it 'basswood'. One of the uses of the wood is in making solid-body electric guitars and basses, which is presumably where it gets its name. The shoots and buds are bright red so that in winter there is a confusion of long brown and red strands on both trees. They contrast with the bright green of the box elder on the other side of the circle. Winter can be a good time to enjoy trees.

American lime leaf

At 10 o'clock we have a **honey locust**, *Gleditsia triacanthos*. Our tree is the variety *inermis* which is without spines. It is an open floaty tree with fresh spring-green leaves that grow in an attractive swirl from the twig. Each leaf has tiny leaflets with no terminal leaflet giving the leaf as a whole an unusual rectangular look. See the write-up on the French Connection above for a note on why 'locust'.

Honey locust leaves and fruit

Closer into the circle and between 6 and 7 o'clock was an American mountain ash, *Sorbus aucuparia*. Shortly before I was due to lead people on my first tree trail for the Heritage Open Weekend, David Curry helped me with some last minute confirmation of tree identification in the American circle. Imagine my surprise when a week or so later I turned to point

American mountain ash leaves and flower

out the mountain ash only to see a fresh stump. I was told that it was seen to be a rather feeble-looking specimen and cleared away, but it may well not have been felled if people had been aware of its significance.

And, finally, we come back to the English oak, *Quercus robur*, in the centre of the circle. The word order on the plaque makes is look as if English oaks are all of American origin. Oaks are so closely associated with British identity that I had thought of them as originating in Europe, but evolutionary studies lead us to believe that they originated in South East Asia around 60 million years ago, which is about 20 million years before India rammed into the continent. Quite recent. The Eocene period was a warm time and the oaks were soon (within 5 million years!) found in China, Europe and North America (Tudge, 2005).

Martin Shuttlewood said that the trees in the American circle are his favourites and when I asked him why he said he liked it that someone thought of doing it.

That appeals to me, too. Good one, Rotary.

Roma Mills' robinia: a tree for radical thinkers

When asked to advise on a tree to honour Roma Mills' term of office as mayor, the first of the new millennium, Paul Arnold chose a *Robinia pseudoacacia*. This time it was not for the tree's French connection but its connection with William Cobbett, 1763 to 1835, the politician, radical and social reformer. It was made clear in the speech to mark the occasion that Cllr Mills was regarded as being radical and social reforming – which is quite an accolade.

The tree is close to the wall round the tennis courts at Batchwood. Is it leaning to the left?

The robinia
planted for
Roma Mills

A London plane for a Westminster horologist

To mark the anniversary of the death of Lord Grimthorpe, Paul Arnold thought it would be good to plant a London plane. This is because Lord Grimthorpe designed the workings of the Westminster clock that we all call Big Ben (the name ought, technically, to be reserved for the big bell in the clock). As a millennium project, a replica of the clock was renewed. It is in the turret at the side of Batchwood Hall which Grimthorpe built and lived in. Grimthorpe's London plane is still not much more than a sapling. It is the small tree right in the centre of the photograph of trees and roses in front of Batchwood Hall. It is bright green against the darker trees behind it and on either side. The sapling destined to be planted broke a limb and another one had to be planted in its stead. You will be pleased to know that a splint has saved the spurned sapling and it has thrived, planted in the woodland close by in Batchwood.

The plane sapling in the centre of the photograph was planted to commemorate Lord Grimthorpe

Alder buckthorn for a battle with firearms

One of Paul Arnold's historical connections that particularly appeals to me is that between Bernards Heath and the alder buckthorn, *Frangula alnus*. The charcoal of the alder buckthorn can be ground to a particularly fine powder and was plugged down into the barrels of hand guns with saltpetre and sulphur to make gunpowder. Hand guns were 'used, probably for the first time in a pitched battle on English soil, at the Second Battle of St Albans' (Burley *et al*, 2007) – which is quite something to commemorate and Paul Arnold did so by planting a grove of buckthorn alder on Bernards Heath.

A great part of the Second Battle of St Albans was fought across what is now Sandridge Road on Bernards Heath. The firearms were worse than useless in the battle: the men were busily fighting before they could load the cumbersome things. They are described as minature cannons held against the chest or under the arm, which sounds more dangerous to the gunner than the enemy.

I cannot find any alder buckthorn on the Heath and would be glad to hear from anyone who knows exactly where it was planted and if the trees have survived. Or go on a hunt for a small bushy tree with no thorns, rounded leaves with a pointed end, small, white, star-shaped flowers that appear in clusters in June, and small round berries that ripen from green to scarlet. It is the food plant of the brimstone butterfly.

A walnut tree for Nathaniel Cotton

Paul Arnold knew that Nathaniel Cotton, an early psychiatrist, had lived and worked in St Albans, and wanted to plant a tree to commemorate him. Nathaniel Cotton and his wife are buried together in St Peters churchyard so that seemed the right place for the tree, and Paul thought of the shape of each half of a walnut kernel and how like a brain it looks and decided a walnut tree would be appropriate.

Nathaniel Cotton is particularly remembered in St Albans for having founded an asylum which he called the *Collegium Insanorum*. It was in Lower Dagnall Street across the top of Spicer Street and, when part of the asylum was demolished to create a link to the new Verulam Road, the link road was called College Street. From maps showing the College when it was entire, we see that it was a substantial U-shaped building with extensive gardens and properly laid-out planting.

Cotton's most famous patient was William Cowper the poet, who suffered extreme depression and came to Cotton in December 1763, leaving in 1765, much restored. Cotton was a forward-thinking practitioner and encouraged his patients to talk through their problems. He also encouraged them to walk, and it is said that Cowper was to be seen walk, walk, walking the streets of St Albans, carrying a lantern if it was after dark.

In the collections of the Linneus Society of London is a letter from Nathaniel Cotton to Richard Pulteney offering to care for a patient for three guineas a week, adding that some patients pay five guineas weekly. Using the retail price index tables, this equates roughly to what we would expect to pay today for residential care of someone with, say, mild dementia. If we use average wage tables, however, we find that the terms would have been unaffordable for a wage earner in the mid-18th century. No doubt Nathaniel Cotton did charitable work – he was a devout Christian active in the non-conformist church – but it would have been mainly the gentry that he catered for.

Cotton's gravestone is the centre one of three lying flat to the earth south east of St Peters church. We can only just make out the words cut into the stone: 'Here are deposited the remains of Ann Hannah and Nathaniel Cotton'. Cotton and Ann (née Pembroke) had eight children and, after Ann died in 1749, Cotton married Harriet Everett in 1751 and they had three children.

Nathaniel Cotton's gravestone is the centre one of three

The walnut tree planted for Nathaniel Cotton is in the low-walled garden to the east of St Peters church. This is the Garden of Hope. It used to be a garden for the blind with a handrail round the edge, and there were sweet smelling plants and benches. The benches have gone but, where they used to be, are recesses in the surrounding low wall. Take the path left into the Garden and then the path across the grass behind the grey stone sculpture, 'God is with us'. Beyond the recess ahead is a four-stemmed tall tree with a pale-beige rough bark and floppy pinnate leaves. This is the walnut tree planted for Nathaniel Cotton.

The tree is said to be easily confused with an ash: the leaves are pinnate like the ash but larger and glossier.

Left: Walnut leaves

Opposite: The walnut planted for Nathaniel Cotton

Walnut catkins appear in spring and are huge, green at first then turning dark yellow.

The scientific name for our walnut tree is *Juglans regia*. All Juglandaceae produce – in their bark, their leaves, their husks and their roots – chemicals called 'juglones' that are noxious to other trees. This benefits the walnut because it hates the shade and needs to be the dominant tree in a group to survive (Tudge, 2005). The 'regia' means royal.

Walnut catkins

Nathaniel Cotton's walnut tree in St Peters churchyard is at the opposite end of St Peters Street to the robinia that started Paul Arnold planting trees for their historical connections.

From the tree planted to commemorate a temple that in some form existed before the Roman occupation to a tree planted for a mayor at the beginning of the third millennium, Paul Arnold's trees represent two millennia of St Albans history.

WILLIAM COWPER ESQ^R

Born 1731.   Died 1800.

Published by J. Johnson, St Paul's Church Yard, January 1806.

Copyright St Albans Museums

William Cowper,
Nathaniel
Cotton's most
famous patient,
© St Albans
Museums

Trees with history

Many more trees than those covered in the previous chapter have associations with past and present people linked to St Albans District. This chapter tells of some of them, and also highlights some old trees which in themselves represent history.

Two cedars of Lebanon for Spencer ladies

Our most favourite tree, the cedar of Lebanon in Sumpter Yard, was planted by the Dowager Countess Spencer on 25 March 1803 (Toms, 1962). On the other side of the Abbey is another cedar and it was planted by the Dowager Countess Spencer's great great great great granddaughter, Princess Diana, when she came to the dedication of the rose window in the south transept. If we look upwards from Princess Diana's tree we can see the rose window.

In another 200 years, perhaps the great great great great granddaughter of Princess Diana will be Queen and come to plant a cedar on another corner of the Abbey.

Lady Spencers Grove

There is a thrilling passage lined with ancient lime trees and horsechestnuts leading from Grove Road on Holywell Hill through to the Abbey Orchard. It has its own street sign: Lady Spencers Grove. To be within it, is like being in a fan-vaulted cathedral: our eyes are taken upwards to the wonderful branching patterns of line and light, lifting us from the mundane.

The Lady Spencer is, again, the Dowager Countess who planted our most favourite tree, the cedar of Lebanon in Sumpter Yard. When her husband John, 1st Earl Spencer, died in 1783, the Dowager came to live in Holywell House which was in the middle of Holywell Hill and the road went round the house where Grove Road is today. The Dowager Countess lived there until she died in 1814 and it is said that she used to use this passage to get from home to the Abbey.

*Opposite:
Cedar in
the Abbey
churchyard
planted by
Princess Diana*

Lady Spencers
Grove

The trees in the Grove are very old. I would like to think that young trees will be planted between the existing ones, and the old ones removed as becomes necessary. It may be difficult, however, because it would be shady for saplings. It will be interesting to see what the experts in the Council decide to do.

Look out for a bullace plum along the Grove, by the way. It has pretty blossom in spring and round red fruits in August.

Gombards yew trees

In 1998, it became apparent that the roots of the yew trees opposite The Spotted Bull in Verulam Road were pushing out the retaining wall, making it unsafe. Initial rough estimates by the Council were that it would cost more

We might have
lost these yews
in Verulam Road

than three times as much to somehow rebuild the wall and retain the yews
and a copper beech tree than to clear and level the site. St Albans people were
upset and some of them met in The Spotted Bull and formed themselves into
the 'Save the Gombards Yews Group'. The wall and the trees behind it were
at the edge of the garden of Gombards House which was where the garages
are now behind the trees. The passageway through the trees is known to local
residents as Gombards Alley, hence the Group's name.

The Group collected 3,000 signatures to a petition, raised funds, put up
posters, obtained extensive coverage in local newspapers and on local radio,
and lobbied councillors. A civil engineer within the Group put forward an
anchoring scheme using metal plates and steel rods which would save the trees

and the wall more cheaply than the Council's first estimate. This scheme was the one adopted and the yews were saved for £14,000.

The participants in the campaign felt that 'a part of St Albans heritage had been preserved just because people were determined not to lose it'. Some of the funds raised went towards sponsoring a tree. See 'The Tree Sponsorship Scheme' in 'Trees and the future'.

A pagoda tree in Abbey Mill Lane

As we walk down Abbey Mill Lane from the Abbey Gateway, we come to a pleasingly symmetrical white house on the right. It is used as diocesan offices now, Abbey Gate Offices, but used to be home to successive senior Abbey

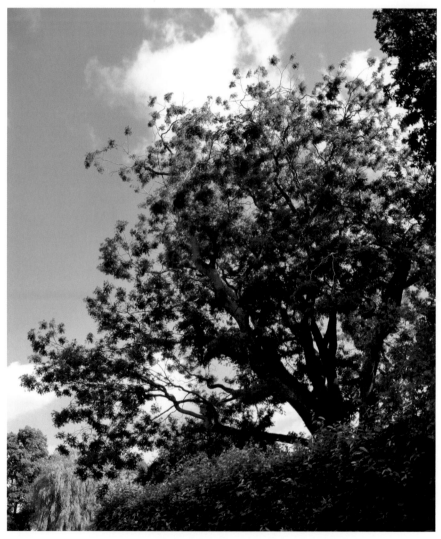

250-year-old pagoda tree behind Abbey Gate Offices in Abbey Mill Lane

THE REMARKABLE TREES OF ST ALBANS

clergymen and their families. In its garden is an old pagoda tree. We can see the tree above the wall and, if we peep round the gate a little further down the hill, can get a glimpse of its graceful spreading form and superbly weird trunk markings. Brian Lee logged it on the Chiltern's Special Tree Project website, www.chilternsaonb.org. There we can see a photograph of the tree taken in 1884. It is an idyllic picture of 'Mr Hales the gardener and his wife and C.S. and J.P. Nisbett sitting down'. The branches of the tree curve upwards in a beautiful shape, a large tree in front of a substantial house and wide garden.

Brian reports that the girth of the tree is 5.2 metres, its height 26 metres, and its age, though no documentary evidence has yet been found, is estimated to be more than 250 years. That takes us back to the mid 1700s when St Albans was beginning to be an important staging post for carriage and horses.

James Gordon is credited with bringing the pagoda tree to Britain in 1753, and Brian Lee wonders if our tree could be one of James Gordon's original specimens. Brian also tells us that the tree has flowered recently – the pagoda tree has hanging inflorescences of creamy white flowers – and is in good shape, which is excellent news.

Crusty bark of the pagoda tree

It was only yards away, in the Abbey Orchard, that another pagoda tree was planted. STAND, the anti-nuclear group, planted it to mark the first British Hiroshima Day in 1985, 40 years from the dropping of the nuclear bomb on the city of Hiroshima in Japan. This tree has not survived so the one in the Abbey Gate Offices gardens must serve to remind us of the day.

The scientific name for the pagoda tree is *Sophora japonica*. It would be appropriate if the genus name were derived from the Greek root meaning wisdom so that we would be reminded that with wisdom we can work out how to avoid war. However, it seems more likely that it comes from an Arabic word 'sophero' meaning butterfly-shaped – which has the positive connotations of beauty and regeneration. The tree belongs to the pea family – as does the robinia that I think it resembles – and the individual flowers could be seen, at a stretch, to be butterfly-shaped.

Despite the scientific species name, the tree originates in China not Japan, but it was often planted in the grounds of Buddhist temples in Japan giving rise to the common name, pagoda tree.

A tulip tree planted by the Queen Mother

A tulip tree planted by the Queen Mother in the grounds of Wheathampstead School

Another tree to be found on a register of special trees is a tulip tree planted in the grounds of what was Wheathampstead Senior School in Butterfield Road, which runs east-west across the top of the hill linking the roads into the village from St Albans and Harpenden.

You can see from the photograph that it is a beautiful tree – and that, in July 2010 when the photograph was taken, it was in a construction site. In due course there will be housing here and the residents will be lucky to have the wonderful tree to enjoy.

A tulip tree for Elsie Toms

It was also a tulip tree that was planted for Dr Elsie Toms who wrote 'The Story of St Albans' and gathered old photographs of St Albans into a fascinating record of 'St Albans as it was'. She lived all her life in St Albans, was head of a secondary school in London and was first elected as a Labour councillor in 1945, was mayor 1960–61, was a councillor and alderman for 18 years, was a founder member of St Albans Civic Society, and worked to retain the character and beauty of St Albans and its surroundings.

The tulip tree was planted in the Abbey Orchard the year Elsie Toms died, 1982. She was 92 years old. Alas, the tree has completely disappeared.

A tulip tree for Jim Greening

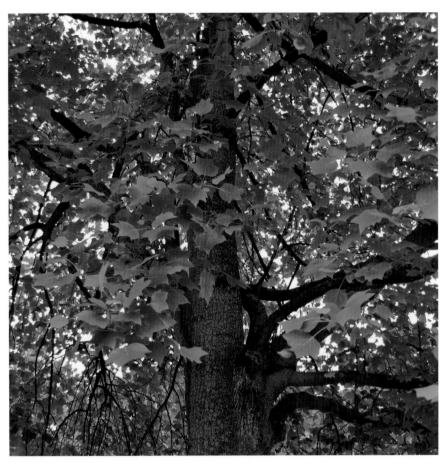

A tulip tree was planted for the last mayor of St Albans City Council, Jim Greening.

Again it was a tulip tree that was planted for another mayor of the city, Jim Greening, the last mayor of the City of St Albans before it was expanded into the St Albans District Council. It is in the top car park outside the entrance to the Batchwood Golf and Tennis Centre. In early June the tulip tree has an unusual-looking flower and, in autumn, the whole tree is a pillar of molten gold ahead of us as we come up the drive into Batchwood.

The tulip tree has a distinctive leaf and flower

I have found that people of all parties speak well of Jim Greening. He and his family were friendly and hospitable. One of his missions was better facilities for the people of the City.

Old hedge lines

Here and there in our towns there is a line of mature oak trees, perhaps interspersed with the occasional ash, which tells us that this was once a hedge line, a field boundary. From aerial photographs we can see how recently there were fields being cultivated or grazed, for example on St Julians Farm. When St Julians housing estate was built, the field boundary must have been kept as a footpath/right of way because we can see a superb line of oaks running all the way from where Butterfield Lane comes through an arch under the Abbey Flyer railway line right up past Mandeville Primary School. There is a particularly majestic specimen in the open space by Holyrood Crescent. It has a girth of nearly 4 metres. Close to the playground, there is also a scrub oak that children clamber over. Who needs brightly coloured metal climbing frames! The real whopper of an oak, not quite on the line, is close to the end of Butterfield Lane in the gardens of Little Sopwell Cottage. One cannot but stand in awe.

On the other side of town, along the east end of Sandpit Lane there is another line of statuesque oak and ash trees and exceptionally fine field maples. Coming in from the east, perhaps from Welwyn Garden City or Jersey Farm, our eyes go to the stunning cedar at the top of the hill and we might not notice on the other side of the road the proud line of trees taking us all the way to the traffic light intersection with Marshalswick Lane and Beechwood Avenue.

Along the edge of London Road, too, there is a line of oaks and then of traditional hedging trees: hawthorn and field maple. And at right angles to London Road, at Kensington Close, there is a line of oaks.

It is interesting to look out for these lines of trees – we see them in Verulamium Park, too – and remember the use of the land, and the generations before us and their occupations in past times.

An oak for adventuring youngsters

A group of youngsters from Verulam and Beaumont Schools went wind surfing on the Mediterranean and were on their way to the Ardeche to do rock climbing and canoeing when their coach driver shockingly and tragically died at the wheel. Some pupils survived the resulting crash without injury, some were injured, many died. It was heartbreaking.

As one of the memorials to the youngsters, parents chose to plant an oak in the quiet of the walled Vintry Gardens in the lee of the Abbey church. As you enter Vintry Gardens from Waxhouse Gate, the oak is directly ahead,

An English oak commemorates young people who were injured or lost their lives in a coach crash during a school adventure holiday

set in the grass a little further down nearer the Abbey. At its foot is a plaque telling the story.

The crash was at Ledignan in France on 29 May 1985. The tree was planted on 16 November of the same year.

A mountain ash for a pioneering lady journalist

At Batchwood in a spot where we can look out over the parkland of the golf course to views of the Abbey, a mountain ash was planted for Beryl

A mountain ash for Beryl Carrington

Carrington who worked on the *Herts Advertiser* for 60 years and was a life-long member of the Red Cross. There is a charming photograph and note about Beryl in James Corbett's 'A history of St Albans'. A mountain ash, or rowan, is a delightful tree with snowy blossom and bright red berries, a good metaphor for a spirited person and pioneering lady journalist. Beryl's tree had a lucky escape when a huge beech tree collapsed, taking with it half of an adjacent oak tree, but missing the rowan.

To find Beryl's tree, we go down the path beside the tower-topped stables alongside Batchwood Hall and then, when we are level with the ha-ha, turn left along the path through the trees. Soon on the right we see the damaged oak with a seat at its base and the beech logs beside it. Beryl's mountain ash is there at the edge of the parkland. Even though the marker with Beryl's name on it was chosen to be so discrete that it would not attract attention, it has disappeared. The great beech logs will be her pointer.

A cork oak for cross-cultural value

It was Donato Cinicolo who took me to see the cork oak planted by his respected friend George Pazzi-Axworthy.

If we go down London Road, pass the Highfield Park roundabout, pass the cemetery on the left, turn next right into Birklands Lane and then almost immediately right again (still in Birklands Lane), we see a right of way on the left. If we go down there, we find ourselves on a track that becomes a footpath. There is a lovely old white farmhouse on the right and, beyond it, a grove with a cork oak and a circle of stone pines.

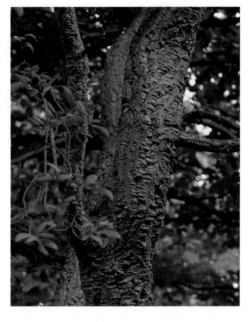

A cork oak in Birklands Lane

The cork oak was planted by George Pazzi-Axworthy when he lived in the nearby old farmhouse. The Pazzi name is a very old and prominent one in Florence. George came to St Albans from Rome and married a Welsh lady. He grew to love Wales and its language and often visited with his family. As a lawyer, his advice was much relied upon by the Italian community among whom he was greatly respected. George's family went on many outings, collecting seedlings of various trees and taking them back to the family home, where they would be planted and lovingly tended. Trees were George's passion.

To me, this tree represents the value that different cultures and communities have added to our District over the years – the millennia.

An ancient yew in St Buttolph churchyard, Shenley

I am stretching a point by including St Buttolphs because, strictly, it is outside the District – but only just, and we do not have another yew of quite this distinction. Its girth is more than 5 metres, 17 feet, making it between 600 and 750 years old (Robert Bevan-Jones in Miles, 2006). It would be neat to say that the tree would have felt the thump of Yorkist feet as the troops trudged to the Second Battle of St Albans in 1461, but they came up from Barnet along Watling Street a good few miles away.

St Buttolphs church is now a private home but the churchyard is open to us. If you go south out of St Albans on Shenley Lane, the B5378, it becomes Black Lion Hill and then London Road. The churchyard is on the left soon after The Black Lion, now a restaurant rather than a pub.

The ancient yew is the big tree on the right of the path towards the house. It is in good form: not a particularly tall tree and with a lovely rounded shape to its crown.

The canopy is dense and the trunk is wonderful with hollows and twists and curves and spaces right through it, the colours warm and varied. The branches elbow this way and then that: I could picture four men lying head to foot along some of them, which makes the branches about 24 feet long.

Looking up into the ancient yew tree in St Buttolphs churchyard, Shenley

THE REMARKABLE TREES OF ST ALBANS

The ancient yew has no fruit, it is a male tree – a male coming into its prime with two or three thousand more years to go. As the millennia pass, the tree will employ strategies to keep it comfortable and regenerate its growth: it will push up new stems; lower its branches until they touch the soil, layer and regenerate; occasionally take a year off, or even a decade, and not grow at all (growth stasis adds to the problems of age estimation); and when its trunk is hollow it might drop some aerial roots down into the vacant space.

The church, now a home, is a fitting backdrop to our ancient tree. The flintwork is knapped (the surface smooth) and squared (each stone is made rectangular) and galleted (splinters of flint have been inserted in the mortar joints for strength). There are rows of larger stones and rows of smaller stones all tightly and neatly and beautifully fitted together.

Other venerable trees

Here and there throughout the district there are lovely old trees. There is the wonderful plane tree at the edge of Verulamium Park; the superb old beech in the Abbey churchyard; the magnificent poplar in the grounds of Kingsbury Mill; the pollarded limes in Romeland; an ash in St Stephens field with a girth of 4 metres, exceptional for an ash; and in Rothamsted Park there are two oaks of 6 and 7 metres respectively.

Once we get our eye in, we find them – and can think about how long they have been there and the changes that have taken place around them.

Opposite:
Ancient yew tree
in St Buttolphs
churchyard,
Shenley.
It was 100 years
old at the time
Columbus sailed
to America

Our favourite trees

There was a good response to our call for people to say if they had a favourite tree or a tree that should be included in a book about St Albans trees.

We found that trees are important to people because of their age, their beauty, their rarity, their links to significant people or events – or because they have personal associations.

Some people had difficulty in limiting themselves to one tree:

Amanda Yorwerth's list

'Hope this isn't too late.

I have a few favourite trees in St Albans – take your pick:

1. **Lombardy poplars** on the south side of the little spur of Cell Barnes Lane that Nuffield Health Club is on. Although on private land, the trees are very tall and easily visible from the road. The best time to see, or perhaps hear, them is in the autumn when hundreds of starlings roost in them and they come alive with birds. When I cycle past them the sound of the thronging birds is a reminder that wildlife is here in St Albans and not just in far-off countryside or on nature programmes on the telly.
2. The spreading **prunus in Clarence park** between the cricket pitch and the park keepers' tool area. There is a bench near it. In mid spring the tree is like a great snow drift – absolutely beautiful. Even better, because the flowers are single, and so prolific the whole tree hums with insects – probably millions of them.
3. **Copper beech tree on the north side of Brampton Road**, near to the top of Blandford Road, in a front garden. An astonishingly big tree in a front garden, with fabulous, burnished, deep-burgundy leaves. How wonderful to see such a magnificent tree in such a suburban road and how lovely that some tree-loving person tolerates it whereas others would have found an excuse to lop or fell it.

Opposite: Pauline Barnes' favourite: a Wellingtonia in Highfield Park

4. Any of the **willows on the north banks of the Ver** near the road bridge next to the Nunnery ruins. Although the river authorities have hacked them about a bit to enable light to get to the river bed, if you look carefully you can trace the branches of these trees back to the main trunk and see the enormous horizontal reach of the branches – quite astonishing and, largely, ignored.

Amanda Yorwerth

The Handley-MacMath list

I am so sorry – my children and I took pictures of the trees we wanted to nominate, but after days of being too busy and the right people who can do digital pictures being too busy, I've given up and must just *tell* you which ones we wanted to celebrate, or it will be too late.

I'm afraid we wanted four – but we're a household of six – so I hope that's OK:

1. As you walk down Folly Lane and pause at the junction with Gombards, ahead in the distance is a field with one beautful, independent, **inconvenient tree** right in the middle of it. We never see it without a sigh of pleasure and relief.
2. We also love the tree – **the only tree – you can see in Victoria Street**, which is mostly hideous and unshaded for commuters ploughing the whole length of it to the station and back. It's one of a group of beautiful mature trees on the corner of Victoria Street and Marlborough Road.
3. We're also very fond of the **trees in Gombards Alley** – the yews in the car park and the magnificent deep red tree near the steps down to the car park.
4. There's a **large tree in Knight's Orchard**. It is one of the few left to us since Chittendens have felled several – and is home to singing birds and a 'lung' to this part of the city. I look at it from my bed from dawn till 7am – again, with relief and great gratitude.

Paul, Tom, and Eleanor Handley
Trinity, George, Terence Handley-MacMath

Amanda Yorwerth and the Handley-MacMaths *were* too late for one of Donato Cinicolo's photographs but we can find their trees and see for ourselves what we think of their choices.

Other trees that people drew to our attention are sometimes included in another section: Paul Arnold's trees, for example. Where this is the case, I have quoted there the comments and mentioned the person who sent them in.

As was done for 'Favourite Trees' produced by Epping Forest District Council and for 'Plymouths Favourite Trees', we gathered a panel to judge which trees should be included in this book. It was decided that all the trees, together with the reasons for their selection, should be included and I hope that you will enjoy the trees and their stories as much as we have done.

A fantastic ash

The ash tree in the garden of a thatched cottage at 1 Lower Luton Road, Harpenden.

Fantastic 150 to 180-year-old ash tree clearly visible from the road.

Tom Thompson

When we went to take a photograph of the tree we found that it had been pruned recently and had nothing like the spreading canopy we can see from Google Earth that it used to have. It is shooting strongly, however, so we can look forward to it regaining its former extent.

Treasure Tots favourite tree, an ash

Over the past six years, our tree has provided the Treasure Tots with

- shelter from the rain;
- shade from the sun;
- a place to climb up, sit in or jump down from;
- a safe place to learn by doing bark rubbings or looking for bugs;
- an interesting view when we hang things from its branches.

Our tree has allowed the children to have fun and it has provided/shared lots of laughter and tears with the children.

Our tree is the oldest member of Treasure Tots.

We hope you agree with us, that our tree is special.
> Parents of the children pictured here and Kim Parker-Mead, secretary to Treasure Tots Pre-School, Colney Heath

How could we not agree that this is a very special tree?

An aspen tree

Mrs Meakin has chosen an aspen (a kind of poplar) in Heath Farm Lane.

> I can see the tree from indoors and outdoors. There is always movement in it and it makes a rustling sound. When I get up at night I can hear it and it sounds as if it is raining.
>
> Mrs Meakin

I like the idea of perpetual sound and motion. It is as if the tree is companionably seeking our attention.

Left: The rustling of aspen leaves sounds like rain falling

Opposite: Treasure Tots Pre-School children under their favourite tree

The drinking tree

One curious characteristic of ancient walls is that they can provide the perfect environment for trees to prosper. So, if you go to Verulamium Park today, you can see portions of the great walls which are almost entirely covered in the woods of the park. One might imagine that some of the trees are the descendants of the seeds dropped by the guarding legionaries.

Only the walls were left behind after the predation of the stone gatherers. The walls were saved because their stones were set in a substance invented by the Romans but not seen in Britain again until the early 20th century: concrete.

Of course time has treated them harshly and what you can see today of the walls of Verulamium represent the product of both modern archaeology as well as the ancient skills of the original construction.

One particular tree has a mythical status for some of those who walk these walls today. Each morning the rain and dew collects in two pools cradled in the roots of the tallest tree in the park. Only in high summer do these secret pools dry up and every dog who walks the paths of the wood knows that there is almost always a cool drink to be found at the Drinking Tree. Legend has it that the spirits of the legionaries look over the animals that drink from these pools, protecting them from the dangers that the walls were built to resist. It is certainly true that there have been no hoards of arsonists from Essex since dogs started to use the tree. That can't be coincidence.

John Gilligan

The tree is on the Park side of the Roman wall not far from Londinium Gate. Once you have seen it, there is no doubt that you have the right tree because the roots have indeed formed a perfect bowl in which water collects. We accosted a dog owner asking if they would mind us taking a photograph of their dog drinking from nature's bowl of water and they and their dog knew all about 'the drinking tree' so John Gilligan and his dog are not the only ones who know about it.

A copper beech that holds the scene together

The copper beech located in the gardens behind the Gonnerston houses on Mount Pleasant must be one of the biggest trees in St Albans and can be seen from miles around but especially from Branch Road, Mount Pleasant and Kingsbury Avenue.

It is my favourite tree because it holds together several completely different periods of architecture by its dominant size and colour.

I can describe the periods of architecture that have a relationship with the copper beech as ranging from the white painted brick of the elegant Victorian Kingsbury Knoll to the uncompromising yellow concrete brick of the sixties Gonnerston. In between these periods and sitting quite comfortably is the quaint part red brick, part chalk clunch of Myrtle Cottage on the corner of Mount Pleasant, the red brick Edwardian houses of Kingsbury Avenue and the stark De Stijl style of the dairy building. Still within sight of the copper beech are the 14th and 17th century barns of Kingsbury Manor and the sober brick-and-tile 1930's Memorial Hall.

Where else can be found so many periods, styles and materials in such a small area as successfully co-habit the spaces around this giant copper beech?

Robert Merrick

These photographs that so well illustrate his observations are Rob Merrick's own.

Childwickbury copper beech for beauty and permanence

Rod Woodward proposed the copper beech in St Marys churchyard, Childwickbury Green:

> A fine well balanced specimen of a tree, clearly seen from the adjacent road or path; complements in colour the brick of the church building. Its presence provides a natural feeling of permanence to the church and surrounding houses, as the human population comes and goes over the years.
>
> Rod Woodward

Botanists tend to refer to the copper beech as 'purple', perhaps because it is only copper coloured in early spring. Later the tops of the leaves do turn purple. At all times it is what I understand landscape architects call an 'accent tree', but the copper is unique and I cannot imagine us changing our terminology.

It amuses me that in the autumn the copper beech turns the same brown as all other beeches. It is as if it repents of its ostentation.

Leaves while they were still coppery

A magnificent cedar and two giant sequoias

The cedar
between two
Sequoia gigantica

Looking up into
one of the giant
sequoias

Just in case they have been missed. They were planted in the 1880s by Henry Bailey when he was building Cuckmans House, now demolished.

Brian Moody

I would have missed them – never dreamt they were there. As I drove to find them along the streets of Chiswell Green I still thought I must be in the wrong place but no, round a bend, there they werein Cuckmans Drive – these three amazingly dominant trees.

St Stephens cedar of Lebanon

The tree has fantastic girth and height. I used to hang around it with
my mates from St Julians (now Marlborough) School at lunchtime.
One time my brother tried to climb it and got stuck and we had to
call the fire brigade. It was really funny because he was about 35 years
old at the time.

Jeff Smyth

We like this tree because it is so old and impressive and full of
character. When we hugged it in 2008, the cedar tree measured 9m or
seven adult hugs! There is also the rumour attached that Henry VIII
courted Anne Boleyn under this tree!

Sandy Norman

It must be the oldest tree in Sopwell. We reckon it is about 500 years
old at least.

Pam Smith

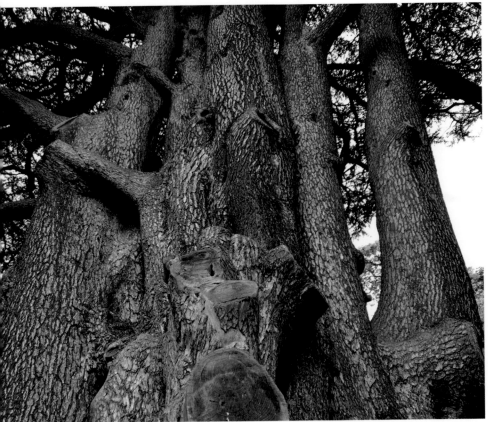

Left: Close in and
looking up into
the cedar

Opposite: The
great cedar of
Lebanon behind
St Stephens
churchyard

Cedars of Lebanon at Gorhambury

I wrote to confirm some facts for this book and Lady Verulam added to her reply:

> Among our personal favourites here are the cedars of Lebanon which we think were planted around 1805. One fell down in the 1990 storm and we counted the rings.
>
> The cedars are visible from the permissive walk and, on house opening days, visitors walk right round them if they choose to look at the garden as well as the house.
>
> Lady Verulam

We see that one of the cedars has a tree house in it so presumably they are favourites for their joy as well as their beauty.

Cedar at St Marys Redbourn

St Marys cedar is my favourite tree because of its lovely spreading branches and the cones underneath. With my friends, I used to collect the cones and paint them different colours and put them in a basket. I see this very old tree and think of the people who have passed under it over all the years gone by.

Stella King

Cedars for remembrance

Mrs Brenda Foster's favourite tree is the cedar of Lebanon on Hatfield Road in the cemetery.

I had not explored the cemetery before and found it neatly kept, peaceful and beautiful with well placed solemn tall conifers, spreading cedars, a lovely avenue of horsechestnuts, and also blossom trees that must be a picture in spring.

The cedar of Labanon that Mrs Foster draws our attention to is near the entrance to the cemetery and close to the railings on Hatfield Road, so that we can see it well each time we pass.

Red and white for the Wars of the Roses

The alternating red and white cherry trees in Sandridge Road were planted to commemorate the Second Battle of St Albans during the Wars of the Roses. The Battle was fought here across Bernards Heath in 1461. White is for the House of York and red for the House of Lancaster.

Four people tell us that these are their favourite trees:

They are such a feature of driving into St Albans in the spring. There is a mixture of the girly pink cherry blossom mixed with the darker red-leaved cherry trees with darker pink blossom, and now some new small trees which are a mottled pink, planted to take over from the older trees as they age. These are along the wide strips of grass at either side of the Sandride Road, called the Wastes.

Charlotte Thorp

The trees cheer you up. It is spring after the long winter.

Amad Purton

The display in spring is spectacular and fine for the rest of the year – and it brings history and the dead to some form of life.

Mel Hilbrown

The blossom on any tree is uplifting but these especially so because of the interleaving of red and white and of old and younger trees – which makes it all last longer. In blossom time I make special journeys and detours to pass the trees and I think of the person whose idea it was, that they thought of us all and our pleasure on into years to come.

Gill Curtis

Left: Not all the blossom comes out at the same time

Opposite: An avenue of red and white blossom for the Wars of the Roses. (I took this photograph: I did not find Donato Cinicolo until after the blossom had gone.)

I do not know whose idea it was to plant the trees, but it was done to celebrate George V's silver jubilee in 1935, which makes the original trees three quarters of a century old in 2010. The trees are steadily being replaced, again with ornamental cherries.

If we want to go native, would alternating red and white hawthorn give the same spectacular effect?

Clarence Park climbing tree

If you enter Clarence Park by the double gates nearest to the bandstand and playground, turn immediately left and walk just a few metres, you will come to our climbing tree. It is on your left opposite some rhododendron bushes.

The tree is an amazing shape with some great low branches for climbing and sitting on. I have spent many a time with each of my three boys when they were little watching them clamber about in this tree – far more entertaining than the playground!

Mary Liming

Sue Howard also refers us to a tree in Clarence Park that children love to climb. Sue says her tree is near the Lodge and she thinks, from memory, that it is a cedar. I think it is the same tree that Mary Liming tells us about.

The tree is a Lawson cypress. See how abundantly dripping down its foliage are its small spherical cones, blue in spring, yellow-green in summer and brown in autumn. After they burst to release their seeds, what is left of the cone hangs on in there. It is fun to take a magnifying glass to the spent cones and see their cubist angles. Male flowers hang at the very ends of the floppy foliage. Tiny and black they fall off when they have released their pollen in early spring.

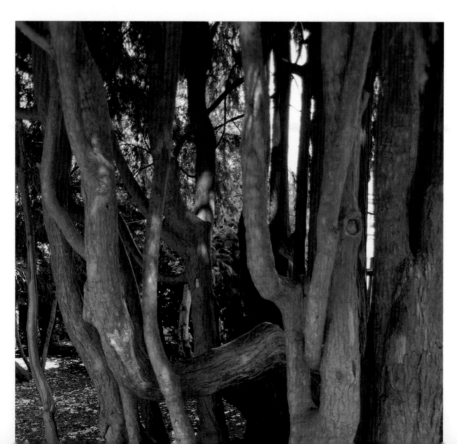

The Cumberland conifer

The conifer in Cumberland Court lawn is my favourite tree because it is a fine example of a mature tree.

Despite buildings changing you can still picture this in the gardens of Borradale.

Note – Borradale is a surname from Cumberland, though John Borradale married Mary Arris on 8th June 1682, at St. Peters, in St Albans, where Mary's father, Thomas, was a doctor and local M.P.

Thomas Arris came from a family of eminent London physicians; his grandfather had been warden of the Company of Barber-Surgeons, and his father, Edward, was sergeant-surgeon to Charles I.

Edward founded the Arrisian anatomy lecture in 1645 and become Master of his company in 1651.

John and Mary Borradale's eldest child, John, was baptised at St. Peters on 13 May 1683, but it appears that the family had moved to Nottingham by 1693 (the date on the present plate) when his twin (?) daughters were baptised at St Nicholas, Nottingham, on 3 August of that year.

David Kaloczi

David Kaloczi tells us that the tree is in what was once the gardens of the large house called Borradale that stood where the Seventh Day Adventist Offices now stand on the corner of St Peters Street and Carlisle Avenue. Cumberland Court is a block of flats along Carlisle Avenue.

A fig tree is a living link with Italy

What precious thing would you take with you if you were emigrating?

When Donato Cinicolo's father came from Italy to St Albans in the 1950s he brought a cutting from a fig tree growing in his home town of San Bartolomeo in Galdo. Whenever the family moved within St Albans, a cutting from the original tree came too.

And now Donato and Rosie also have a 30-year-old fig tree in their garden where it flourishes and bears fruit. It provides a living link with Italy.

What an heirloom.

A venerable horsechestnut

The horsechestnut on the corner of Station Road and Harpenden High Street is a fine old tree with widespread branches and deep foliage. Every year it comes into bud a couple of weeks before all the neighbouring trees and when it comes into leaf you know that spring is really on the way. As Geoffrey says it seems to lift the heart. No one seems to know why this tree is the first to flower. Some say that its roots reach down to the stream which runs under Harpenden Common at this point, others that it grows in what was once a farmyard fertilised with centuries of manure, or that it is on the site of an old abattoir! Whatever the truth it is a delight to see every year.

Maggie and Geoffrey Turner

The tree is braced by cables, which is just as well because children are often to be seen clambering around its lower branches – and gown-ups after a few jars seem unable to resist trying to climb up into it.

See how knobbly and interesting the bark is.

Chime Square horsechestnut

This tree is my favourite because it is a magnificent specimen of *Aesculus hippocastanum* (horsechestnut to you and me!) and must be about 80 foot high and is now [May 2010] festooned with beautiful white 'candles'. When I was a child I planted a 'conker' and was thrilled when it grew into a miniature chestnut tree. I now wonder what happened to it when we moved house. And to think that this specimen started in the same way – incredible!

From the Latin name I conjecture that Spanish castanets are made from horsechestnut wood. It can also be used to make toys, in cabinet-making, packing cases, and, in the old days, milk pails because of its whiteness. It is also sometimes used to make charcoal.

The name comes from the horseshoe-like marks to be found under the fat brown buds.

Pat Shea

This has to be the best example of a horsechestnut in springtime. It is a huge tree and the branches radiating out from the sturdy trunk have a wonderful display of 'candles' flowers. No doubt hundreds of conkers in the autumn. I do not know its age but it was always there when the bus garage was in use – before Chime Square was built!

Alison Chant

This tree is my favourite because of its great beauty, its size and all the changes it has seen over the years:

The beauty comes from the changes over seasons. In spring we have the fresh new leaves with the petalled flowers resembling 'candles' or small lupins. The large showy leaves of summer, leading to the 'fruit' which gives us our conkers. Winter shows us the bold shape of its strong structure.

The tree's size is such that people walk under it without appreciating its massiveness. It stands there, a symbol of power, defying anyone to try and move it.

This item could have been called 'Where have all the buses gone?' as our tree has seen so many changes over the years. At one time queues formed nearby as people waited in summer to board the 'special' buses to spend the day at Whipsnade Zoo. We had Green Line buses (712 Luton to Dorking; 713 Dunstable to Dorking) pulling in at

Opposite: Horsechestnut in the gardens of Chime Square on St Peters Street, the photograph taken in early morning light and before inevitable heavy traffic has built up

St Albans Bus Garage, as well as the L.T. bus No. 84 to Arnos Grove, which terminated here. Then we had our own Country buses: the 313 to Enfield, the 368, 369 to Dunstable whose home base was in the garage in the shadow of this wonderful horsechestnut.

So long may this beautiful tree stand tall and add glorious autumn colour for the pleasure of many generations of St Albans citizens to come.

Jim Mullany

... because it is so huge.

Anthony Nicholson

It raises my spirits. The tree looks magnificent in Spring when the 'candles' of flowers are in bloom.

There used to be another horsechestnut, even larger, which was shamefully allowed to be cut down by developers when the flats were built.

Cathleen Palmer

The Chime Square horsechestnut spreads above adjacent buildings. The tree was here in the time of our bus garage before Chime Square apartments were built.

St Stephens horsechestnut

The magnificent horsechestnut located in the churchyard of St
Stephens church adjacent to Watling Street, girth approximately 5.35
metres, height approximately 20 metres.

Reg Beer

We like this tree because it is so old and impressive and full of
character and must have witnessed several historic occasions as well as
hundreds of weddings.

Sandy Norman

It is so very old and a magnificent specimen of horsechestnut. No one
is quite sure how old it is – but I think it is worthy of a mention in
the book.

Mrs Nancy Walker

Geoff Dunk tells us that the horsechestnut tree in St Stephen's churchyard
was planted on 22nd November 1785 (Dunk, 1985). We do not know the
reason but we can picture the people who gathered round in knee breeches or
wide skirts and powdered wigs. There has been great change since then.

See also 'St Albans city churchyards' for a full-page photograph looking up
into the tree.

A lone horsechestnut

I like the thought of hot hazy summer days sitting on the bench
whiling away the hours. I like the thought that perhaps women in
past times on an afternoon off could sit here too and relax. I imagine
them on their own. I think it each time I pass.

Sarah Terry

The tree that inspires thoughts of peaceful solitude is on a path between The
Swing Bridge pub on Southdown Road and the duck ponds on Harpenden
Common.

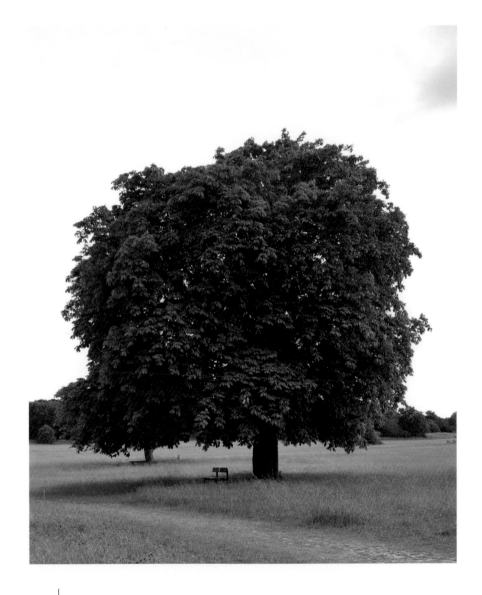

THE REMARKABLE TREES OF ST ALBANS

An Indian bean tree on the Highfield tree trail

I lead Health Walks around Highfield Park and this tree always causes the most interest and we have to tailor our walks to keep an eye on it throughout the seasons.

Sue Hawkins

Below is a photograph of the leaves and last-year's beans on the tree in mid summer after flowering. The flowers are similar to the candles of a horsechestnut but larger and more open. In 2010, this tree finished its flowering earlier than the Indian bean tree by The Silver Cup in Harpenden and earlier than the one in Clarence Park. Try in early July for flowers but, as Sue Hawkins says, keep coming back at different seasons to enjoy the shape alone in winter, the great big floppy new leaves in late spring and the pendulous elongated beans throughout the year.

St Michaels Manor lime tree

The lime tree in the grounds of St Michaels Manor is my favourite
tree because it changes with the seasons, is a home for birds, and is
unashamedly large. I suspect that it is the tallest tree in St Albans.

Roger Sansom

You can see the tree as you walk up Fishpool Street. It is my favourite
tree because, when I am walking home from the Six Bells at night and
see the tree in the dark, the top branches look like two people kissing.

Well, they do to me!

Deborah-Jane Hilda Kishman

This tree was one of the 'Twelve Trees of Christmas' in 2003. It was 'dressed'
by the Italian community of St Albans, and Guides and Brownies sang
traditional songs. I wish I had been there.

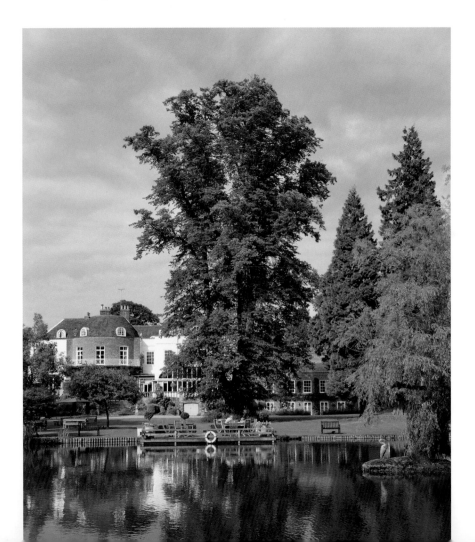

The mistletoe lime in the Abbey Orchard

John Rae wrote me a letter that I treasure. Here is a reproduction of a sketch that he included:

Dear Kate, I told you about the tree beside (below) the Abbey where all the girls of St Albans stand beneath the mistletoe every Friday night.

John Rae

Oscar Wilde said 'I never, ever, exaggerate.'

A magnolia in the heart of St Albans

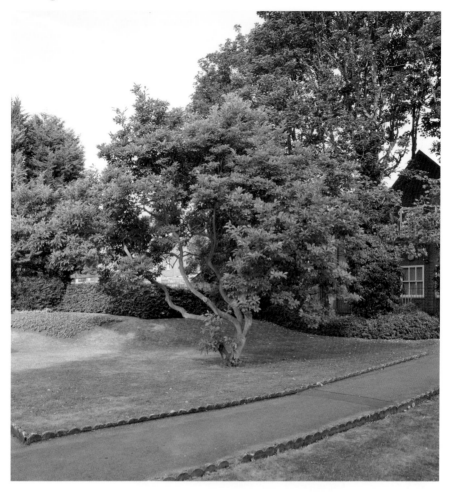

The magnolia tree in the little park behind St Peters Street, Hatfield Road
and the Council offices is my favourite because it is such a wonderful
sight when in bloom and so close to the busy centre of town.

Laurie Gibson

Magnolias are particularly spectacular because their flowers are out before the
leaves so that in April we get the whole shape of the tree as a mass of nothing
but flowers.

It amazes me that magnolia trees are considered a possible candidate for
being the first of flowering plants to evolve: the first of angiosperms (Tudge,
2005). The flowers are so large and impressive that intuitively one feels that
they must have evolved well after those plants with less extravagant flowers.

THE REMARKABLE TREES OF ST ALBANS

Variegated maple

My favourite tree is a variegated maple down Waxhouse Alley, St Albans, where the alley opens out to the north east of the Abbey and the path curves round following the old vineyard wall. I love the old flagstones, the old lampost, and the light shining straight through the windows of the choir. But most of all I love the maple tree.

It is my favourite tree because of its beautiful shape and colour, and the way it enhances one of the loveliest places I know. I love to see this tree as I turn down Waxhouse Alley leaving the noise of the street behind, or coming the other way up the slope from the Abbey. The strong slim trunk and the perfect crown of leaves – a startling bright lime green in spring, and a gorgeous deep crimson in autumn. Even in winter I love its perfect form. I love its brilliant colours after rain or early in the morning, at night by lamplight or on a stormy evening. It is a picturesque spot already but the tree is the focal point of the corner, bringing life and colour.

Andy Davies

....because it interestingly has two types of leaf. One is very bright yellow/green, the other darker green. It is very good at the moment.

John Rae

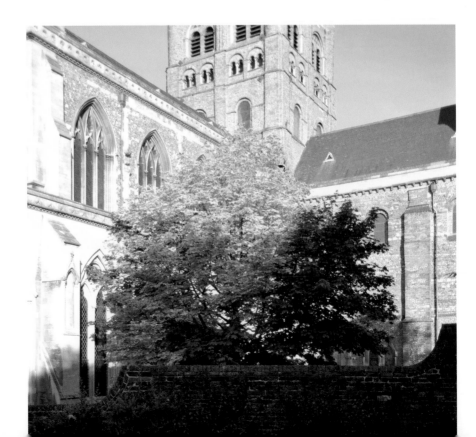

A medlar

Nick Edmonds submitted as a favourite the medlar tree in his front garden in Cunningham Avenue, St Albans.

There is a medlar in Old Welwyn that has a plaque against it saying that it may be the only one in Hertfordshire so that it is good that we have one here.

The fruits look like tiny monkey skulls and are only edible once they are rotten. The tree originated in Persia and used to be popular in English Victorian gardens for its gothic effect: not only are the fruits skull-like but the trees look gnarled and ancient and interesting even in their early years.

Medlars are self pollinating and do not grow too large so perhaps they will become more popular again in today's smaller gardens. We would be well advised to learn what the Victorians knew: to wait until October to pick the fruit and then to leave it to 'blet' or until it 'reaches the bletting stage' – for which read 'has gone rotten'.

Monkey puzzles

The monkey puzzle opposite the Sunrise Café in Southdown is my favourite. Neighbours hang monkeys from the branches which makes us laugh as we are sitting having a coffee in the café.

Robert Naylor-Stables

The fact that someone has hung monkeys on the branches is what appeals to Elliot Tate, too.

Clare Raynor tells us that her favourite tree is the mature female monkey puzzle in her garden at 37 Queens Crescent, Marshalswick. The tree is in the garden behind the house but is just about visible from the street.

The monkey puzzle, *Araucaria araucana*, originated in Chile and Argentina. The way the whorled shoots all curve upward gives the trees a confident jaunty look which I find appealing.

Sander's Mexican lime

The tree in grounds of St Albans and St Stephens School, Camp
Road, behind No. 47 Camp Road and opposite Cecil Road, is
important to the history of this area. It was planted in about 1886 by
Frederick Sander, 'The Orchid King', whose orchid nurseries then
occupied this site. In recognition of Sander's links with the Royal
Botanical Gardens at Kew, he was presented with one of three such
trees in England. (The others are/were at Kew and Chorleywood
College.) This Mexican lime carries a 'TPO 42' protection. Its
winter skeletal form is beautiful and in summer its unspoiled form
impressive, culminating in an aromatic climax in August.

Tony Billings

The Mexican lime foliage is extraordinarily dense, pale underneath and
brighter green above.

The flowers are prolific and pendulous. Above each flower cluster is a
bract that looks like a slender leaf. It curls upwards and outwards adding to
the vivacity of the tree.

Copper beeches for Sander's sons

Tony Billings has given me permission to quote from his book 'The Camp':

> Today it is difficult to believe that Sander's orchid empire ever existed;
> all that remains is a group of trees which he planted.... Just below
> [the Mexican lime] is what appears to be a single lofty copper beach;
> actually it is a group of three trees Sander planted to mark the births
> of his sons Fritz, Fearnley and Louis.
>
> A sole red hawthorn marks the entrance to the Sander house.
>
> Billings, 2002

The red hawthorn has gone now. It went when a wicket gate into the school
grounds was inserted opposite Vanda Crescent a few years ago. But the
wonderful trio of copper beeches is here for us to admire.

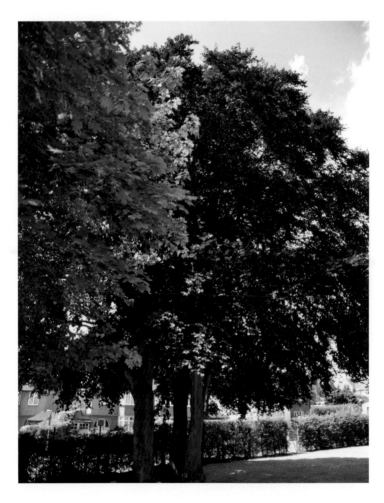

An oak on the edge of Wheathampstead's oppidum

A majestic oak on the right hand side of Beech Hyde Lane as you go up the hill from Marford Road, Wheathampstead, is my favourite tree. It is around 400 or 500-years old and situated in the middle of what was a very big Celtic–Catuvellauni settlement marked on the map as 'Belgic Oppidum' (Belgic City).

The country lane sneaks around this special tree: a marker of time past, present and future in a landscape that has changed little in over 2,000 years. It also grows close to where the chieftain's palace was thought to be.

These are all reasons why this is my special tree. It is a tree of wisdom.

Neil Sankey

Beaumont oaks

The tree in the rear garden of 63 Woodland Drive, St Albans, is my favourite tree. It is tall enough to be seen from the street (and of course from Google Earth!) and is probably the oldest tree still alive on the former Beaumonts Farm and already a mature tree when the original Beaumonts Manor was still standing in the 17th century.

I was born and brought up next door to the former Beaumonts Farm (near where the manor had been) at 57 Woodland Drive and the oak was part of my life as my bedroom was at the back of the house. Its enormous branches spread wide and almost over the roof of the nearest house. Today this would not be allowed and a park would be laid out around it, but before the war the developer/builder took no notice of such things and there were fewer regulations.

The tree was home to bats, red and then grey squirrels, owls, and a variety of other birds. The sound of leaves rustling in high winds was distinctive.

Some time after 1960 the tree surgeons were called in and spent the day clipping the main branches in an attempt to reduce the risk of damage to the house if a branch should fall. I still miss the form and life of the tree as it was before lopping.

Mike Neighbour

Vic and Vera Foster live next door to the tree, and its branches spread right across their garden. They say that the tree is like a metropolis with every kind of life within it.

At the other end and on the other side of Woodland Drive is a sibling oak which is the favourite tree of Mary Robey in whose garden it stands guardian.

Left: The oak at
63 Woodland Drive

Opposite: The oak
at 6 Woodland
Drive

A pair of oaks in a vicarage garden

My favourite trees are two aging oaks, both with TPOs, both showing their age. One is particularly notable in its old age for hosting two other trees in its trunk: a laurel, and a rowan tree that is currently in flower and will bear berries in due course.

Mark Slater

The trees are in St Lukes vicarage garden, Cell Barnes Lane, St Albans, clearly visible from the side of the church.

One of the trees is a living miracle: a miracle because it is living. It has a decent canopy of leaves, especially considering its great age which is obvious from its girth, but it has only a ten-inch-wide strip of bark under which to get all the nutrients and water it needs to sustain that canopy.

Not only that: the tree has these other trees living off it. It was strange to see the rowan leaves amongst oak leaves on one side of the tree and laurel amongst the oak leaves on the other side. Each tree seemingly thriving.

Is our calm dignified tree showing us how little we need in order to be alive, that we should ask no more than to be alive, and that we can nurture whoever comes our way even if they are different from ourselves? How apt a metaphor for a vicarage garden.

Earlier pollarding has created a podium about 2.5 metres off the ground and Donato Cinicolo said, 'This tree needs somebody in it.'

'A vicar?' I suggested.

Mark Slater was up for it and went to put on a dog collar and get a ladder. Up he climbed and cheerfully posed for the photograph.

The second tree of the pair is equally venerable but has most of its bark intact so it looks more comfortable. I felt glad it was there to lend support to its companion. A fanciful thought, of course, because no doubt they are competing for nutrients.

I like the swing hanging between the two oaks: a sign of young things enjoying old things.

Oaks make a shady glade for a sunny Sunday morning

My favourite trees are the young oaks close to the Kohima Epitaph in Jersey Farm Woodland Park. The trees have recently become large enough to sit under on a hot day. We can look over the open fields and surrounding woodlands whilst keeping out of the sun.

The light breeze that the trees seem to produce beneath them even on a hot and still day is perfect for relaxing and appreciating the big skies and vibrant colours of the different trees and grasses.

Having an epitaph in such a beautiful position adds to the charm of the spot for me. When I look across the field or walk down to Sandridge I never fail to feel very lucky to be able to share this woodland and my favourite tree freely within the neighbourhood in which I live.

Anita Wall

The Hatching Green oak

As we go down Redbourn Lane from Harpenden towards Redbourn, the road curves gently left so that we see ahead of us a huge oak tree. It is on the corner of High Elms where the road begins to curve smoothly right.

> In its close juxtaposition with a lovely house in a residential environment this tree reminds us of the dignity and wonder of nature. May it endure, perhaps even outlasting the house.
>
> Ric Andrews

I do not know about the house, but the tree ought to outlast you and me.

There is an altogether attractive sweep of trees here: first there are exceptionally tall ash trees above laurels and conifers, a weeping willow, the magnificent oak, a lovely spreading cherry tree, a balsam poplar and then another weeping willow. The fragrance of the leaves of the balsam poplar is aromatic.

St Albans Museum oak

A group of local residents, including historians, scientists and
eminent politicians, were involved in the campaign for a museum in
St Albans. It took fifty years to come to fruition but eventually the
Hertfordshire County Museum (as it was then) opened in 1899.

Many objects were donated by local collectors. One of the most
touching gifts of all was a sapling from the Great Oak at Panshangar
House, Hertfordshire, which was donated by Earl Cowper. It was
planted in the opening year and is now a mature oak tree.

I love this tree because it is so full of life and steeped in history.
When I look at it I am reminded of the people who campaigned for
the museum. I think of their pride and fascination with the history
and archaeology of the area. I think of them in their straw boaters
planting the little sapling, knowing, even hoping, that it would outlive
them.

Elanor Cowland, Keeper of Community History
at Museum of St Albans

The Panshanger Great Oak was visited in 1789 by Gilbert White, author of
'*The Natural History of Selbourne*'. He lived in Selbourne in Hampshire so that
it was something of a pilgrimage to come all the way to Hertfordshire. He
commented favourably on the 'form' of the tree. I wonder whether then it
had allowed its lower branches to rest on the ground. Certainly Jacob George
Strutt tells us in his '*Portrait of Forest Trees*', published in 1822, of the branches
dipping down to the very ground (Morton, 2004).

The Great Oak is still there but can only be visited by appointment with
Lafarge Aggregates.

The gardens behind St Albans Museum, on the other hand, are open to
us all and are a delight. They were laid out consciously to foster biodiversity.
There is a pond and flowers and pathways – and our own Great Oak.

Nomansland climbing tree

It is known as 'the climbing tree' and some of the branches have been worn smooth by climber after climber climbing its branches.

Alex Laurie

I wondered if the climbing tree on Nomansland Common has been nominated? It's loved and smothered by small children all summer and looks amazing.

Sue Howard

When we went to take a photograph of the tree there were indeed children clambering over it. A father had brought his little ones over from Hatfield. He said that he has often met mums and dads who say that they used to climb on the tree when they were children and now bring their own family to enjoy it.

See how low the bottom branches of the tree are.

To find the tree from the Nomansland car park, cross Ferrars Lane and walk left under the trees to an open meadow. The ground slopes down and then up to a simple bench. Go down the slope and then to the right where you will see the climbing tree ahead.

London plane in Catherine Street

Ted Petts nominated the London plane tree in Catherine Street outside what we all call Bleak House but ought now to call Dalton House.

> About 35 years ago, I lopped and felled the beech tree that was there before because it was dead and dangerous. It was replaced by the plane tree and I have watched it grow over the years and love it.
>
> Ted Petts

How bleak that junction would be without Ted's lovely spreading plane tree.

Silver Cup plane trees

Belinda Naylor-Stables likes the trees beside The Silver Cup in Harpenden.

> These have beautiful prickly 'conkers' towards the end of summer.
> The leaves also turn wonderfully in the Autumn. The branches look
> fantastic against the sky.
>
> Belinda Naylor-Stables

It is usually horsechestnut fruits we call 'conkers', but plane fruits in their cases are equally spiny – and stay hanging on the tree like Christmas decorations.

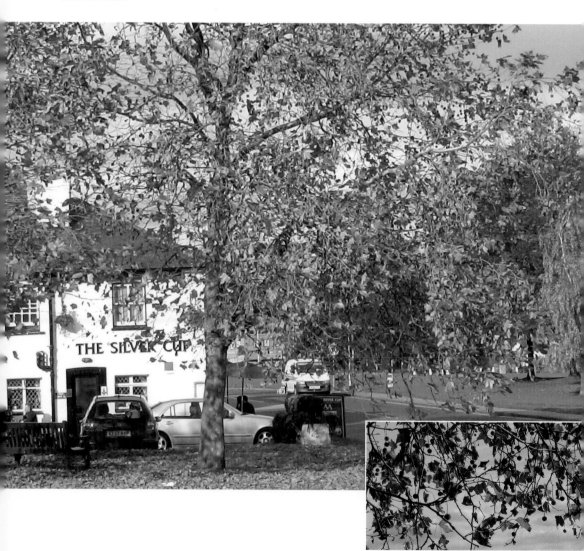

Plane perfect

My favourite tree is the plane in Bricket Road, St Albans, at the side of the police station. It shows how important large trees are in the urban landscape.

Like others of its kind, it survives in about as hostile an environment for a tree as can be imagined: in the centre of a city, in a car park, surrounded by concrete with cars parked for the best part of each day as close to its trunk as they can get. Yet there it stands unpollarded, spreading its branches to obscure one of St Albans most unlovely buildings, helping to purify the air, providing shade and a home for wildlife, stately, beautiful, it lifts the spirits. It's a delight to the eye. Long may it remain!

Penny Jones

Penny's plane tree is not only at risk from pollution and compacting: it is one of a pair of planes and they, a copper beech, a silver birch and a liquid-ambar are all within a plot which is up for development.

Can we hope for an imaginative architect who could make the planes the centre piece of an open-arched courtyard, the copper beech and silver birch and liquidambar outside its walls?

Look out for the softly fountaining silver birch, enjoy the changing colours of the liquidambar, and admire the copper beech, knowing we might not always have the benefit of them. The copper beech at risk is the one shown below. It is on the corner of Bricket Road and the road to Waterend Barn.

A plane to be seen from afar

The plane admired by Patrick Remmington is on the edge of Verulamium Park. It is in the gardens of a house in Fishpool Street but is so close to the river that it seems to be in the park. As you come in to the park from the entrance by the bridge in St Michaels Street, the plane is in amongst the glorious bank of trees on the left. It is far and away the tallest of them.

> It is a huge and magnificent example with a nice shape including large lower branches which must compare very favourably with any London plane in the centre of London. I see and admire it every day whilst walking the dog and think it deserves some recognition after taking what must be 250-plus years to grow.
>
> Patrick Remmington

Patrick Remmington is not the only person who admires and salutes the plane: when I was walking the 'Cycle Ride for Historical Churches' with Norman Lavers, he pointed out the plane to me. He said that whenever he was near, he would make a detour to see the tree – as I have done ever since. Mr Lavers died this year, 2010.

Here is a photograph of the tree taken from within its garden in Fishpool Street. For a photograph looking up into the tree, see 'Verulamium Park'.

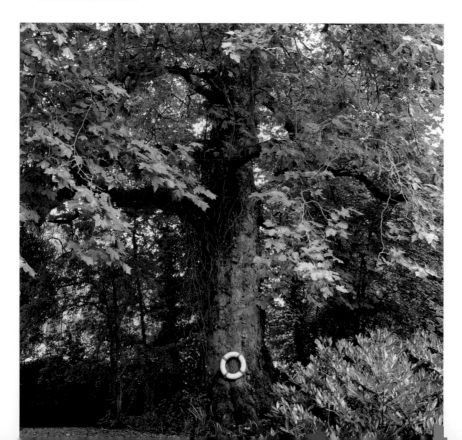

Prospect's prunus and The Limes limes

In the gardens of flats 54-68 Prospect Road, St Albans, is a pair of trees
of an unusual kind I have not seen elsewhere. Many people admire
them. There were three trees, but they were drastically over-pruned in
1998 and one died as a result. They have pretty delicate pink blossom
which comes early, followed by red leaves like a copper beech, then a
round fruit like a big cherry but with flesh and stone like a damson.
Birds love eating the blossom and ripe fruit. One tenant told me they
were a Japanese tree and the fruit was inedible, another that the fruit is
edible if boiled for a long time. Passers-by pick the fruit so I don't think
it is poisonous, just not sweet. I have long wanted to identify these trees,
and, if I move, I would like to grow them. I moved to St Albans in 1986
and the trees were mature then. The flats were built in 1929 so the trees
are probably 30 years old.

Maxine Elvey

The lime trees at the entrance to The Limes are my favourite trees
because they are beautiful – a lovely green – and they are such mature
trees, and a landmark.

Carol Mulberry

A beckoning pine

Whenever I am walking home from the town up to Mount Pleasant, however I am feeling, the tree sort of pulls me up the hill, and says to me you're nearly home. Even when it drops all its needles and I slip on them, I don't mind – it's a beacon.

Ann Hollowood

Pine with a beautiful shape

My favourite tree is a pine in the garden of No. 97 Fishpool Street viewed from outside 122–130 Fishpool Street as you go down the Street on the raised pavement. It is my favourite because, although we cannot see the whole of the trunk, we can see the beautiful colour, textured bark and, above all, the elegant shape of its needles against the sky. A beautiful thing.

Madeleine Sansom

Matched poplars

Along the Ver in the Gorhambury Estate is a plantation of poplar trees. They can be seen from the Redbourn Road (A5183) and, if you walk along the section of the Ver Valley Walk that is a permissive path through the estate, you walk under them.

> For me, the trees are a link with the past: they remind me of how things used to be when most adults, my dad included, smoked cigarettes and used matches to light them. I have been told, you see, that the poplars were planted under the guidance of Bryant and May as a crop for making matches – but that by the time the trees reached maturity the bottom had fallen out of the market: lighters came along, and that was that for matches. Most of the trees have been left to grow on but some of them were felled in 2008. I wonder what their timber was used for. We shall miss the trees along the river if they all go.
>
> Anne Valentine

The poplars are truly beautiful – in different ways depending on the light.

Lady Verulam confirms: 'You are quite right: the poplars were planted for the matches market which then collapsed.

'We also have cricket bat willows along the river so, despite the felling of the poplars, there are and will be plenty of trees there.'

Both poplars and cricket bat willows have a faint blue to their green, the willows almost grey, nestling against the taller poplars further along.

There is also a line of lofty lime trees along that Gorhambury side of Redbourn Road. They are closer to the road, level with The Pré. They, too, are superb.

High tree in Highfield

It is a beautiful tree, approximately 30 metres in height (about 100 feet) – rooted in my neighbour's garden but dominates my own garden and can be seen from some distance away. I believe that it may have been planted in the second half of the 19th century, when Wellingtonias were fashionable with the Victorians.

Pauline Barnes

This tree would have been planted at least a hundred years ago in the grounds of Hill End Hospital.

I love the way the foliage curls upwards and the cones swing gaily. In July the cones looked pale green from afar but were already made up of browning lozenge shapes outlined in bright green.

THE REMARKABLE TREES OF ST ALBANS

St Nicholas matched pair

A giant sequoia stands at each end of St Nicholas church in Harpenden town centre. The towering trees are visible from Church Green and Kirkwick Avenue – and from within the churchyard.

> They are prime specimens of the species (*giganteum*). An estimate
> of their height is 100–120 feet and they are virtually identical. They
> cannot be more than 150 years old as the species was only brought to
> the UK in the mid 19th century.
>
> Andrew Smith

'Wellingtonia' is one of the names for the *Sequoiadendron giganteum*. Others are 'Sierra redwood', 'giant sequoia', and 'big tree'. The first seeds came to Britain in 1853 so it is not surprising that John Lindley of the London Horticultural Society named the tree *Wellingtonia giganteum* in honour of the Duke of Wellington who died the year before (Miles, 2006). Its name contributed to the tree becoming a 'must have' for grand Victorian gardens and parks.

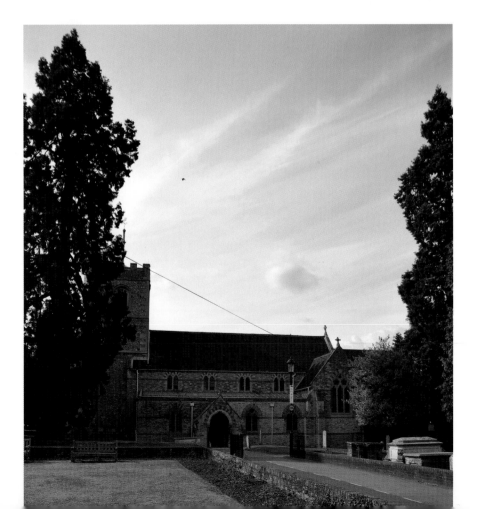

Soaring sequoia in Sandpit Lane

Lisa Curry wrote to say that her favourite tree was the redwood in Sandpit Lane in front of the flats in The Dell. I asked her whether she could say why she had chosen it:

> I suppose I love it just because it feels so out of place! The huge, beautiful redwood in the middle of St Albans. I often wonder why it's there, if it got planted or if it just seeded the natural way and how old it is? It's a mystery! I suppose that's why I love it. I love the colour of its bark as well, that deep red colour is lovely.
>
> Lisa Curry

These redwoods are certainly tall! See that this one is twice the height of the three-storey building behind it.

A sweet chestnut in Hill Street

From Verulam Road, drive down Hill Street in the next few days and, when you reach the place where you could park motorcycles, look left at the big tree 'in flower' now!

THAT's my favourite, at my favourite time of year for it.

Veronica Furner, on 9 July 2010

I am not sure why Veronica put 'in flower' in quotation marks. Could it be that she does not want us to expect something showy? To those unfamiliar with a sweet chestnut, the long creamy green strands might look as if they are foliage.

The tree is well set back behind the house but visible when you know where to look. Now that we do know, it will add to our pleasure when we walk along Hill Street.

A wide-spreading sycamore

When I asked a man whom I had met when he was doing charcoal burning whether he had a favourite tree, he drew my attention to this splendid sycamore that has been given the space to spread into its full natural range. It is on the corner of Waverley Road and Batchwood Drive – a busy junction of the ring road round St Albans – but I had never noticed it before.

I notice it now.

The scientific name for a sycamore is *Acer pseudoplatanus*. It is the same genus as maples and has large lobed leaves and flaky bark similar to those of a plane (*platanus*).

If you ever have time, walk up close to enjoy the wonderful patterns of the bark. And look up into the tree.

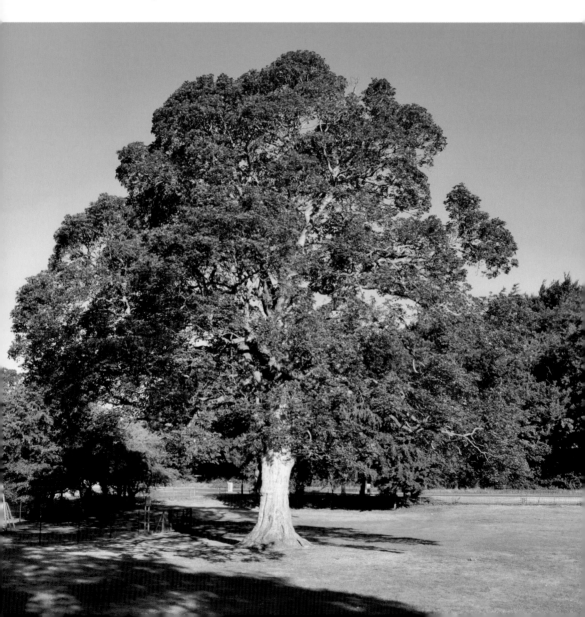

The Duke of Marlborough weeping willow

I have chosen the weeping willow at the bottom of Holywell Hill because a childhood friend had a willow in their garden and I used to like going through inside. The leaves fell like a curtain and it gave me a magical feeling – like being inside a cave – completely surrounded by tree.

Kate Shuttlewood

Willows are unusual, especially for a tree with catkins, in being insect, not wind, pollinated. This is a good adaptation because male and female willow catkins are on separate trees so that pollen blown by the wind might well not find a female willow catkin. Bees, on the other hand, can find the next source of nectar anywhere within a few miles and the chances are, at that time of year, it will be another willow. One drawback of insect pollination for early flowering trees is that insects need warmth to get them going. Willow fertilization therefore depends on sunny days in March.

Weeping willow in Verulamium Park

The tree was a lovely little refuge for us when we were at St Michaels primary school. The leaves used to come right down to the ground so we would sit under it without being seen by the outside world! We used to sit and swing on its branches (without damaging them of course – we were very small!) for picnics and chats. It was a perfect little den for us :)

Lucy Crick

Lucy Crick and her friends are not the only ones to have loved playing under the willow skirts:

The willow tree is really beautiful. It is fantastically big and looks wonderfully peaceful and serene as you enter the park. It then however reveals a secret self and becomes a source of great fun for our family as the children love to run under its branches and play peek-a-boo, hide and seek, etc. We just think it is a great tree that looks spectacular and is fantastic fun. It has been there as long as I can remember and creates a lovely introduction to great parkland.

Jane and Dan Mountain,
members of the Cunningham Avenue Residents Association

The willow is on the right-hand side as you approach the lake from the Waffle House entrance to Verulamium Park. It is in fact three trees whose foliage makes a perfect outline, as of a single tree.

Yews in the station car park on Ridgmont Road, St Albans

In particular, it is the two yew trees in amongst a line of other trees, each fighting for elbow room, that inspire Philippa Parker:

> They are fine examples and are clinging on in this unbeautiful location, surrounded by cars. I hope they have preservation orders on them.
>
> Philippa Parker

Ivy is smothering some of the trees and they are all battling for light. The cedar's answer is to spread over the road, further softening the hard cityscape for us.

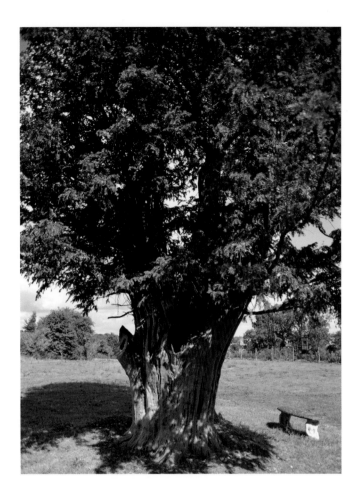

A yew at Norrington End

The yew tree in the garden of the house next door to us in
Norrington End is my favourite tree because it is very old and has an
unusually positive shape for an English yew. Its girth is 4.7metres.

Kate Bretherton

On a bleak gloomy day in winter, it gives me a different
perspective on life. Over the centuries our yew has seen
it all: gloomy days like this come and then they go. My
neighbour, Steve Mills, gave me one of his photographs
that shows the yew on just such a day.

Trees that are history

Before the Grand Climax of St Albans most favourite tree, it seems right to tell of trees that are no longer there but are important enough in people's minds for them to write in and tell us about them. Peter Burley is one of the authors of 'The Battles of St Albans'. He wrote in to say:

> I think the most famous (perhaps the only famous) tree in St Albans is one that no longer exists and we don't know exactly where it was. Nonetheless I would commend giving it a mention. It is an oak tree, probably near the King Will, under which Henry VI sat obliviously singing hymns to himself while the Second Battle of St Albans raged around him on 17 February 1461. It does conjure up quite an image.
>
> Peter Burley

Have you heard before the phrases 'eye-sore', 'safety hazard', 'in the way of the traffic'? There is nothing new. These were the reasons given for 'clearing away' an elm in Hatfield Road. When? 1907. The headline in the *Herts Advertiser* of 20 April 1907 was 'Last of the Mohicans'. The article referred to it as a 'traditional tree' and mourned its passing, but pass it did. At one time there must have been a number of elms in Hatfield Road and, to be called 'Mohicans', must have come to be bare-branched sharp-pointed remnants of their former selves. Mark Freeman, author of 'St Albans, a history', nominated this tree for inclusion.

> Many years ago there used to be a large tree in the middle of where Hatfield Road, Clarence Road and Camp Road meet, forming a roundabout. I can't remember what kind of tree it was, but it made a huge and wonderful impact on that area. There must be pictures of it somewhere.
>
> Penny Jones

I can find no pictures of the tree. I wonder whether anyone else remembers it – and whether it was one of the 'Mohicans' and had to come down because it was diseased.

> Whichever way the sun is shining when the tree is in leaf it beckons like a shining beacon between the two fields.
>
> Pat Beaumont

Penny Jones tells us that Pat's copper beech is in the Napsbury Lane end of the hedge between the two fields at the back of Ayletts' Garden Centre on the A414, that it has been dying for some time (large amount of bracket fungus) and is now quite dead, and very unsafe. Strictly speaking it is on private land: the fields were the subject of a recent village green application by the local residents. Whatever the verdict on the open space, it sounds as if it is too late for the copper beech, but I so loved Pat Beaumont's description of the tree that I wanted to share it with everyone.

Although members of the current St Albans Mothers Union claim no knowledge of this next tree, Jim Cozens' description is so graphic that I want to share it, too:

> I came up to town one day for one reason or another and I saw
> groups of motherly-looking women – each group with a banner
> like the ones we see in church or carried by trade union members –
> processing up from the Abbey to town and round the old Town Hall.
> The procession was slow and silent and had power and impact. It was
> very impressive.
>
> Jim Cozens (born 1926)

My son Richard characteristically gave me his *least* favourite tree. It, too, no longer exists but he would not want not to hold on to the fun of his resentment against it. And he is not the only one, it seems, for the tree is the reason that St Albans City Football Club was denied promotion.

> During a second spell in charge [John Mitchell] took the Saints to the
> runners-up position in 1992–93 only to be denied promotion to the
> Conference at that time due to a 140-year-old oak tree standing within
> the terrace behind one of the goals. In 1998 the diseased tree was
> felled.
>
> www.sacfc.co.uk

St Albans most favourite tree:
the Abbey cedar of Lebanon in Sumpter Yard

More people nominated the cedar of Lebanon in Sumpter Yard close to the
Abbey as their favourite than nominated any other tree. It is an iconic tree:
often, people would tell me about a personal favourite and then say 'and of
course the Abbey cedar'. People tend to say the 'Abbey' rather than 'cathedral',
I notice.

The tree has conflicting associations: one with the Abbey as all-embracing
church of the martyr, the other with superstitious rituals that are unexpectedly
widely known and long practised.

... as a well known and very public tree.

Jenny Faldon

It is a symbol of St Albans' history. Alban gave his life to save a
Roman soldier – and became the first English Christian martyr. He
was executed because he confessed his Christian faith. The tree is over
200 years old.

Anne-Marie Dawe

We nicknamed it 'the wishing tree' as you're supposed to hold your
breath as you walk under its branches and make a wish. You're not
allowed to breathe again until you've cleared the tree's branches (this
sometimes means having to run the last bit if you haven't taken a
large enough lungful of air!).

Lucy Crick

If you walk round widdershins (anti-clockwise) 7 times, you will see
the devil.

Carol Mulberry

It's almost too obvious to mention, but I think this tree is magnificent!

Jan Lennon

...its age and beauty

Pam Smith

This is the bewitching tree. When you run around it anti-clockwise at
midnight on Hallowe'en three times you get to see all the ghosts and
undead of St Albans past.

Ivor Kellock

This tree has magnificent spreading branches which remind me of
a mother duck spreading out her wings inviting her ducklings to

Opposite: St
Albans' most
favourite tree:
the Abbey cedar
of Lebanon in
Sumpter Yard

come in and seek shelter and warmth. This tree seems to me to be inviting citizens to come and seek shelter and warmth in the church (cathedral) and its environs.

Richard R Blossom

In the early 1930s we children were told not to speak under the tree because it would be unlucky. It was a tradition. Perhaps it was a way of preparing the children to be quiet when they went into the church. It was also said that if you walked round it 12 times at midnight, horrible things would appear. Of course, none of us was up at midnight.

Jim Cozens (born 1926)

We were told at Hallowe'en that you must be quiet as you go under the tree or an evil spirit or a ghost would come out and get you. If you did make a noise, you would be safe only if you ran round it three times clockwise absolutely silently. Even now that I am 29, I still think of the story when I go past.

Steven Brooks

It provides a picturesque setting for our cathedral.

Reg Beer

I've attached some photos I took of it in December 2009 (the tree covered in snow) which I hope will explain why it is my favourite – but in words – ancient, majestic and almost part of the Abbey itself.

David Chadwick

Here is one of David Chadwick's photographs.

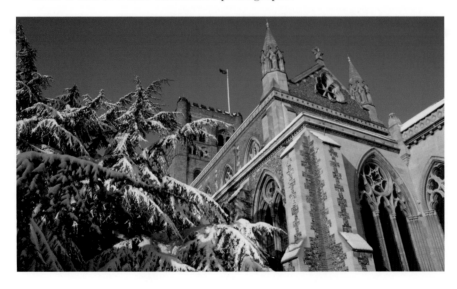

Here are two more detailed photographs of favourite trees.

Leaves of the variegated maple nominated by Andy Davies and John Rae. The tree is in the passage from Waxhouse Gate to Sumpter Yard.

A branch of the oak tree nominated by Neil Sankey. It is on Beech Hyde Lane, Wheathamstead.

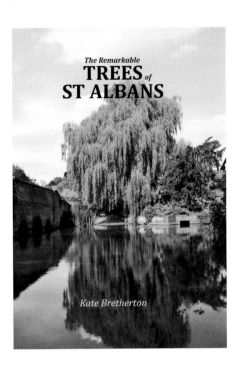

The Remarkable
TREES *of*
ST ALBANS

Kate Bretherton

Would your group or organisation welcome a talk on trees?

"The Remarkable Trees of St Albans"
or
"How to recognise and remember which tree is which"
or
"Trees and our local history"
or
"What keeps trees upright?"

For more information contact: Kate Bretherton
01582 791912 or 07901 945920
kate@walk-talk.co.uk
www.walk-talk.co.uk

St Albans city parks

St Albans has remarkable parks: snug little places tucked right into the heart of the city, one beside the Council Offices behind St Peters Street and Vintry Gardens behind the High Street; Clarence Park with its collection of Victorian specimen trees; the incomparably beautiful Verulamium Park in its lakeside setting and views of the Abbey above banks of trees; Victoria Park which is a model for community enterprise and commitment; Jersey Farm Woodland Park, which has lovely open countryside; Bernards Heath with its wilderness, woodland, parkland and open fields; and Highfield Park with its mix of one-hundred-year-old trees and new planting.

Vintry Gardens

Vintry Gardens is down Waxhouse Gate right in the heart of St Albans between the High Street and the abbey. It is a walled garden and, until the 1970s, was the garden of a house in the High Street.

> 'Incidently, I always liked the *Ginkgo biloba* tree in the Vintry Gardens, it seems a bit out of place...'
>
> Elanor Cowland

Who could not like a *Ginkgo biloba* anywhere. The common name is 'maidenhair tree' and it has a delicate pretty look with its special deeply-incised fan-shaped leaves, soft and velvety in whorls round each spur. The *Ginkgo* in Vintry Gardens is mature and magnificent. The interesting thing is that these fabulous trees are madly primitive. They are gymnosperms like cycads, yews and conifers. 'Gym' is from the Greek word meaning naked – ancient Greeks were naked when they did their workouts – and the seeds of gymnosperms are not clothed in an ovary as is the case for other trees, angiosperms. Another phrase I like in this context is 'motile sperms do the fertilizing': the distinction being that the pollen tubes of angiosperms have to burrow through living tissue down to the seed in the ovary whereas the pollen of gymnosperms 'exhibit [their own] motion'. There are fossil records of

Ginkgo biloba tree
in Vintry Gardens

Mulberry tree in
Vintry Gardens

THE REMARKABLE TREES OF ST ALBANS

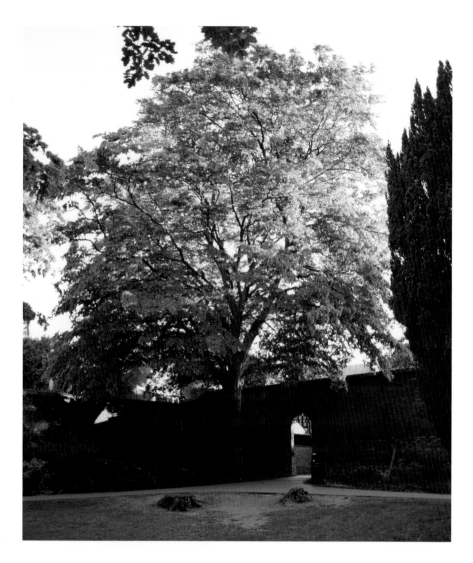

Hornbeam in
Vintry Gardens

Ginkgoales 260 million years ago when the continents were still snuggled up
together as one great supercontinent, Pangaea. Remember that fossil records
of oaks only go back 40 million years when all the continents were where they
are now (Tudge, 2005).

Vintry Gardens is a popular place for people to go at leisure times. There are
seats and lawns and wonderful old yews trees, a walnut on the Abbey side, the
golden ash in the top corner planted for the 'Year of Prisoners of Conscience'
(see 'Paul Arnold's trees'), the attractive oak planted for adventuring youngsters
who died in a tragic accident (see 'Trees with history'), an amazingly large
hornbeam in the corner by the upper entrance and a wonderful old mulberry
tree that bears good flavourful fruit. A path winds down via rounded steps
through herbs to the lower gate out into Sumpter Yard.

Clarence Park

If you were a millionaire, what gift would you give to the people of your town? Something that would be for everyone now and forever? John Blundell Maple gave us Clarence Park in 1894. He bought the land from John Poyntz, Earl Spencer and a bit from Frederick Sander, the orchid grower (see the Mexican lime in 'Our favourite trees'), 25 acres in all. He bought 11,000 trees and shrubs from W Paul & Son in Waltham Cross, 300 species in all. He commissioned the local building firm of Miskin to build the pavilion and the lodge. He had laid out a cricket pitch, tennis and quoits courts, a football field, a bowling green and cinder tracks for running and cycling. He put in six hydrants to water the cricket pitch, and his wife, Lady (Emily) Maple, gave us an Aberdeen granite drinking fountain. Then as now, access to the park was free but people had to pay for using the sports facilities.

An avenue runs from the bandstand to the fountain

There is an avenue of maples, venerable planes and oaks from a bandstand to Lady Maple's fountain. The whole area around the avenue is the part of the Park devoted to specimen trees and there are some here that are seldom seen except in public parks: an euodia, a foxglove tree, a tree of heaven, a weeping ash and an oriental hawthorn.

The euodia, *Tetradium daniellii*, is in the corner by the 'away' gate of the football ground. It does not look frightfully impressive after drastic pruning, but no doubt it will come back to its full glory. The tree originates in China. It is famous for having no leafbud casing – the tiny folded leaflet is surrounded only by dense red-brown hairs. An attractive thing about the euodia is that it flowers in autumn. After the drastic pruning, the only limb that carries flowers is very high but if we look up we can see fist-sized clusters of deep red flowers. And that is in September.

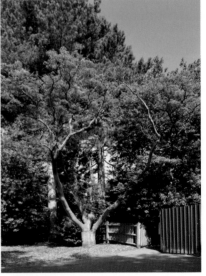

An euodia

The foxglove tree, *Paulownia tomentosa*, is the one with a sloping trunk close to the path that runs alongside Hatfield Road. It is next to an Indian bean tree. Both have floppy leaves and pale flowers in large panicles but the foxglove leaves have an extra point midway along opposite margins, the flowers are earlier (May not July) and are more mauve and the fruits are in heart-shaped cases rather than the long thin pendulous pods of the Indian bean tree.

Foxglove tree trunk and seeds and Indian bean tree flowers

Between the Indian bean tree and the avenue is the tree of heaven, *Ailanthus altissima*. It has pinnate leaves, red on opening and then a lovely fresh green. The leaves are larger than those of an ash and each leaflet has a pair of pointy little lobes at its base.

Tree of heaven foliage and detail showing its crimson petioles

The oriental hawthorn, *Crataegus laciniata*, is only as oriental as Sicily. Its leaves are a prettily incised downy grey, and its fruits are downy orange-red. The one in Clarence Park is next to the tree of heaven.

The weeping ash, *Fraxinus pendula*, is impressive and is what it says on the tin: dense ash-like foliage fountaining out and down as does a weeping willow. It is alongside a bed of yellow roses over near the lodge.

Weeping ash

There are umpteen varieties of maples throughout Clarence Park, as one would expect when Maple was the surname of the man selecting the trees. Some of the leaves are deeply incised, some have hardly discernable lobes, some have great big seeds with wings spread across in a line, some have small seeds in a horseshoe pattern, some seeds are green, some seeds are red, some petioles are crimson, some petioles are yellow, some leaves are fresh green and some leaves are purple-brown, some trunks are smoother than others, some bark has twisting patterns. I would not want to spoil your fun trying to make out which variety is which – but take some headache tablets as well as your field guide.

Deodar branch tips droop. Dawn redwood foliage is dainty.

There are good examples of Atlas cedars, especially the ones by the lodge. There is a lovely deodar cedar with its languidly drooping branch tips on the lodge side of the bandstand adjacent to a conical dawn redwood.

There is a restaurant on the corner of Clarence Road and Hatfield Road and it opens on to the Park where we can sit out at tables. A waterfall of a grape vine over the walls and purple prunus trees round about make it pleasant. Next to the prunus trees and in amongst maples is a silver lime, *Tilia tomentosa*. It is a real wow! Dense foliage, silver grey underneath, abundant flowers and great height make this tree exceptional.

The silver lime contrasts with the greens around it

The photograph frontispiece of this chapter is of a tulip tree in Clarence Park. It is near the basket ball net not far from the zigzag up to Hatfield Road. It is a truly wonderful tree in every way. Lord Maple himself took some trouble to position it where it would get the right amount of sunshine and his care has been well rewarded. There is another tulip tree in the Park, within sight of the first, close to the fountain and within the avenue. Tulip trees have a distinctive leaf shape which reminds me of the

Tulip tree leaves

simplified dress shapes I cut out of paper as a child to fit round a cardboard doll. It is worth our while to find the tulip trees and admire them from afar and to look up into their divine heights. In autumn the whole tree becomes a tower of molten gold.

There is another special tree in Clarence Park. This time it is not in the area of specimen trees but at the corner of York Road and Clarence Road. It is a wych elm with a girth of nearly a metre and a spread the width of Clarence Road. It arches right up and over us as we drive along oblivious of being under an elm tree. Wych elms are relatively resistant to Dutch elm disease and this one shows no sign of being invaded. Andrew Branch, head of Trees and Woodlands at the Council, pointed me to the tree but how I had missed it is hard to imagine. I was fascinated by the early pretty maple blossom on trees along York Road but entirely overlooked the giveaway heaps of elm seeds in the gutter.

We nearly lost our elm. When I marvelled to a friend about it he said that he had been asked to look into the problem of the awkward camber in the road at that corner. On inspection it was obvious that the tree and its root system caused the hump but my friend advised that nothing should be done about it because the awkward camber calmed the traffic speed and increased rather than reduced safety. Life can take interesting turns.

I have described just some of the trees in the Park. There are red oaks

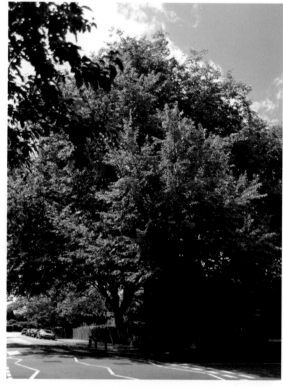

Wych elm in Clarence Park on the corner of Clarence Road and York Road

and red horsechestnuts, whitebeam, thujas and Lawson cypresses, stone pines along the Clarence Road fence from the lodge to the restaurant, an exquisite liquidambar near the pavilion, trees planted in commemoration: masses of super trees for us to enjoy – a truly remarkable park.

Opposite: looking up into one of Clarence Park's tulip trees

Verulamium Park and Westminster Lodge

Wherever we took my late father–in-law, he had always been somewhere better. Not so with Verulamium Park. "I have never seen a lovelier park than this, Kate," he said in his measured Lancastrian voice.

Before we go into the Park at the entrance by the river in St Michaels, it is worth looking over the road to the far end of the Kingsbury Mill car park. The poplar there is amazingly tall and wide spreading.

As we come into the park we see a group of willows, wide and fountaining up and out and down. This group is seen as one tree and is a great favourite (see 'Our favourite trees').

Away to our left on the edge of the river towards The Blue Anchor is a row of drastically pruned willows – they looked like stumps last winter but they have a bit of shape again now.

There follows a dense bank of trees along the edge of the river. See if you can pick out a plane tree amongst them, and go in under the branches and you will find you are on the edge of water on the far side of which is the huge

Left: Poplar by Kingsbury Mill. This photograph is taken from the far side of the tree across the Ver.

Opposite: The four larches growing along the line of the Roman wall in Verulamium Park are iconic.

Looking up into the great plane tree

trunk of that plane tree. Then look up – and up, and up to see the extent of this amazing tree. As you come out into the light you will be able to see the top of the tree above all the others. This is another of 'Our favourite trees'.

Look also for two conical-shaped trees with delicate fern-like foliage. These are dawn redwoods, *Metasequoia glyptostroboides*, and are, for me, one of the prettiest trees I know.

There are more lovely willows ahead on the edge of the lake, one weeping on the near side of the bridge and then a goat willow on the further side of the bridge.

The lake and bridge and dense bank of trees along the river

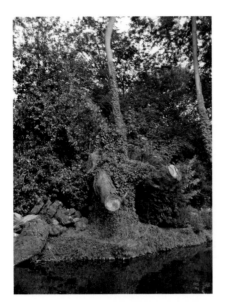

Tidying by Friends of Verulamium Park has left one stump looking like a person

There is a wonderful array of horsechestnuts, ash, sycamores and maples sweeping up and sometimes swooping down over the river. The Friends of Verulamium Park tidy this stretch when it shows signs of getting totally out of hand. We can see some of the results of their work in sawn-off branches and piles of logs left for beetles important to the cycle of nature.

There is a whitebeam and a beacon of a Scots pine on our right and then many grey willow trees that look good from the other side of the lake, their light colour a foil to the rich green foliage behind.

At the end of the lake, we turn and walk along the lower level of the causeway, enjoying the reflections of the picturesque willow-covered island, a remarkable heronry.

As our path curves upwards to the left, there is an insignificant looking tree but I have my eye on it. It is a hawthorn and has good space around it which is unusual for a hawthorn, even in the countryside, where they are usually part of our hedges. I hope I am around in twenty years time to see how it has shaped itself.

There is a remarkable heronry on the island

Through the trees to our left is Westminster Lodge. If we divert up the path a little we will be surprised to see quite a shrubbery and three robinias. This was the garden of the farm house that used to be here. Whoever lived here would have had a wonderful view of the Abbey. If we raise our eyes we can see the generous bank of trees, mostly poplars along the bank of the Ver, and see, also, a group of poplars and willows round a modest brick building in the middle of the field.

Retracing our steps to the path we were on, we continue in the direction we were going, leaving the lake behind us to go up the incline towards the fencing round the foundations of the Londinium Gate of Verulamium. Horsechestnuts, limes and sycamores soar high to left and right on either side of the Gate.

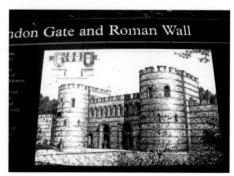

A horsechestnut towers as high as Londinium Gate must have done

The trees give us a measure of the height the wall and entrance gates must have been: on the Roman wall leading away from us we can see the layers of flint and mortar between rows of terracotta tiles. If we count the towers'

The line of Watling Street

layers in the picture on the information board, and add them in our imagination to the layers in the existing wall, we can see that the gate would have been massively impressive – as tall as our massively impressive trees.

There is a pathway behind the Gate that crosses the extraordinarily deep ancient ditch. Watling Street to Londinium would have run from here to where St Stephens Hill meets King Harry Lane at St Stephens Church and then on as straight as a die to what is now Marble Arch. If we go a little way through, we come to one of my favourite trees, a mature sycamore of splendid shape. Below the sycamore to our left is the circle of American trees planted to commemorate the founding of Rotary International in Chicago (see 'Paul Arnold's trees planted for their historical connections'). Above us is the Abbey View golf course with its striking trio of copper beech trees and pretty curved plantings of wild cherry, lovely in the early spring, and a good mixture of other broadleaf trees.

A mature sycamore

Trees on the edge of the Abbey View golf course

Returning to Londinium Gate and skirting its railings, we take the path behind the Roman wall. Gangly trees arch out towards our path. They are wych elms and, in April, have a mass of seeds that look like flowers. Feel how rough the leaves are. That is characteristic of the elm.

Elm seeds in April

The drinking tree mentioned in 'Our favourite trees' is on the slope of the Roman wall on our left, and from here on, within the curve of the wall, are wonderful specimen trees, well spaced so that they have reached their full height and spreading natural grace, or grouped in magical groves.

THE REMARKABLE TREES OF ST ALBANS

There are deciduous trees: oaks and beeches, planes, sycamores, maples and dainty hornbeams. The branch-bones make exciting patterns in winter, each with their distinctive leaf buds: pointed brown-red of the beech, small multi-bumps of the oak, swollen and green of the sycamore, slender and irregular of the hornbeam. In March there are swathes of yellow carpet from maple flowers, in April pink from beech blossom. In May there is still the tracery of branches on some trees, the tender copper of beech leaves, silver for grey willow and poplar underleaves, and fresh spring green for some others. In summer the trees are magnificent in their fullness, and in autumn the colours are spectacular: golds and reds and browns.

Beech trees in early spring – and a detail of maple flowers and copper beech flowers

And in amongst the deciduous trees are some very special evergreens. We come first to a group of tall cedars. There are four true cedars. For current purposes, we can ignore the Cyprian cedar because it is not grown much here. The others are the cedar of Lebanon, the Atlas cedar and deodar cedar. Even according to Alan Mitchell's field guide (regarded as the bible for tree identification), the foliage of the different species of cedar is indistinguishable except at the branch tips. A supposed clever way to remember which is which is L for Lebanon and level, A for Atlas and ascending, and D for deodar and descending. We are not talking about the branches as a whole but of the new shoots – the very tips of the branches. All the cedars have barrel-shaped cones with a whorled indentation in the centre of the top. They are apple green in spring gradually growing more pink and then brown. It is a joy to unravel them after they have fallen to the ground. They come apart into lovely shapes, wide at the top then curving in then out then down to a point. They are velvety to the touch, tawny outlined in brown with a pale line across the wide part.

Opposite: In summer, a grove of copper beech trees is magical

Cedar trees

Consultants employed by the Council identified this first group of three as cedars of Lebanon, the distinguishing feature of which is the way the branches of mature trees form layers – making them utterly stately – as we know from our churchyards. Vic Coombs identified these three as deodar cedars.

The next evergreens are a pair of giant redwoods, *Sequoiadendron giganteum* one much taller than the other, both with their distinctive conical shape. The two trees are down in a bit of a hollow, which lessens the effect of their height. They have dense foliage and splayed and buttressed bases that will become more so with time. See if you can find a cone. They are egg shaped, the size of a hen's egg or bigger, and I think they look as if they are covered in kisses from wide-mouthed 1950s puckered smackers.

In their area of origin, the slopes of Sierra Nevada in America, some of the trees are more than 3,500 years old. We do not expect trees here in England to be as long lived – but who knows.

A pair of giant redwoods

Giant redwood cone

Note that the trunks of the giant redwoods are unusually squashy and fibrous. They are fire resistant and the seeds in general only germinate after fire. The scenario is something like this: terrible fire, all trees around burnt to a cinder, sequoia seeds burst from their cones onto ash-fertilised soil and start germinating in the ground below where there is lots of sunlight and no competition from other species. If the parent tree does die from the fire, all the better for sunlight for the seedlings.

Upwards from the sequoias towards the Roman wall are three superb Douglas firs. They have cheerful upward lilting branches counter to one of the distinctive features of Douglas firs: the downward hang of their cones and yew-like foliage, soft to the touch. Another distinctive feature of this fir is the cones which have three points on each scale.

Distinctive 3-point scales of a Douglas fir cone

Douglas firs are the tallest trees in this country. It is a native of North America but cultivated throughout Britain for its high quality timber. Here protected in the park, it might reach its estimated life span of 750 years (Coombs, 2004). What a wonderful legacy we leave for the generations to come.

The Latin name for the Douglas fir is *Pseudotsuga menziesii*. 'Pseudo' means false, and the English common name for *tsuga* is hemlock, not the poisonous herb, but a similarly towering pine with yew-like foliage. Menzies is the name of the man who first discovered the trees in British Columbia in 1792, but it was David Douglas who successfully brought back the seeds from North West America in 1827, hence the common name. The seeds were nurtured at Scone and a tree from one of those seeds survives today.

Douglas was a great character and intrepid specimen gatherer and kept an account of his adventures for us to read. He tells us that he risked his life in appalling weather, fell down a ravine, capsized in rapids, clashed with North Americans and several times nearly starved to death. But his end tops it all: he accidently fell into a bull pit in Hawaii and was gored to death. He was only 35 years old (Miles, 2007).

Look on our Douglas firs, marvel at Douglas and know that Douglas fir masts and spars have sailed the oceans and the trees have changed forestry in Britain.

The wide-spreading conifers that we come to next are six excellent Atlas cedars.

The first of them is a blue Atlas cedar but the ones on the other side are not so grey-blue in colour. The branches are wonderfully wide-spreading and the tree tops echo the peaks of the Atlas mountains from where they originate.

The scientific name for the Atlas cedar is *Cedrus atlantica* and it is also called the Atlantic cedar. The blue variety is var. *glauca*, one of the most planted of all decorative conifers.

Opposite: Douglas firs

Along the left side of our path has been the curving line of what was the Roman wall, densely wooded with beech, ash, oak, sycamore and maple. If we go up onto the wall alongside the Atlas cedars, we see the amazing network of the roots of beech trees. The prominent remains of the Roman wall come to an end with a huge beech. If we go round to the far side we see across a slope down and then up to a line of mature trees interspersed with such smaller hedging stuff as blackthorn (white with its pretty blossom in March), hawthorn (white with mayflower in May) and elder (cream with umbrate flower heads in June) all along King Harry Lane. If we go up to where there is a gap in the line, we see an amazing tree stump as wide as I am long. It must have been an absolutely massive beech tree. We can see the substantial logs from it on the ground nearby.

Atlas cedars have wide-spreading branches

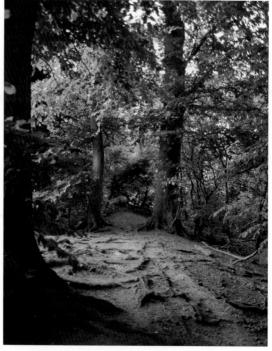

Roots of beech trees on the Roman wall

The stump of a beech tree is as wide as I am long

As we turn our backs on King Harry Lane and look over the Park we have a breathtaking vista of wide grassy space, mature standards, the lake below, the bank of trees above it up to the town, and the Abbey far right. We are fortunate to be here.

The Abbey from the top of the Park in autumn

As we walk down the hill, we note how the trees ahead are in a line across the park. These mark old field boundaries. See how the whitebeam stands out pale against the oaks, beeches and sycamores on either side. At the far end of this line of trees, beyond the white hypocaust building, are the stone pines planted to commemorate

Whitebeam foliage is pale grey

the Roman temple (see 'Paul Arnold's trees planted for their historical connections'). The stone pines have a distinctive umbrella shape which marks them out from the other pines around them.

We cross the line of trees only to see another line across ahead. In this line, away to the left, is a single larch in a line of good, spreading, sycamores, and an especially majestic sycamore on the boundary. This turns out to be a pair of sycamores whose canopies have spread to make them look like one tree. Their bark has formed beautiful swirling patterns.

Ahead is the hedge round Verulamium Museum car park, which is an absolute picture in spring with luxurious bowers of dense white ornamental cherry blossom.

On the left, just through the hedge, is the ladies gate into St Michaels churchyard and through the car park is Verulamium Museum.

However, if we turn to walk along the path on the park side of the hedge, we can explore more of the Park. When we come to a path by the tennis courts we can turn left towards the Inn on the Park, and on down towards

Cherry trees in the Verulamium Museum car park in April

the lake. Along the lake side we shall find a soaring double-crowned lime tree, a prettily shaped silver birch, a wonderfully ancient London plane allowing its lower branches to sag, a super group of horsechestnuts, six beeches – two green, four copper – and, near the play pool, a group of maples and then a group of cherry trees.

And so we reach the lake edge and have to choose our path home.

Jersey Farm Woodland Park

Open countryside in Jersey Farm Woodland Park

Jersey Farm Woodland Park is an idyllic stretch of open countryside and woodland between Sandringham Crescent and a field short of Sandridge. A board at the entrance, where Chiltern Road joins the Crescent, tells us all about the history of the area and that '10,000 trees have been planted including 800 as a millennium project in November 1999. 16 London planes have been planted at the four entrances. Among the trees planted here are alder, ash, beech, crabapple, holly, hornbeam, larch, lime, oak, pine, poplar, silver birch, and sycamore.'

Not only are there the trees listed above but also hawthorn, blackthorn, cherry and rowans in a great wild bushy hedge. Within the shelter belt of the trees and hedging, grass stretches away, with white daisies or whichever meadow flowers are in season, giving us long views over to Sandridge.

It has been a most successful use of land for the community, the trees protecting the Park from traffic noise and pollution – a great big natural open space for us to enjoy.

Victoria Park

I could take a bet and be sure to win that at least half of the people reading this will be wondering which is Victoria Park. And yet we all know it. It is the triangular space above the point where Verulam Road and Folly Lane meet. There is a garage together with a tyre and exhaust fitter right at the point and then the Park.

Victoria Park in evening light

It might seem like a bit of left-over space, an awkward shape, difficult to do anything with, which was just left open. Not so. There was a plan to move Aboyne Lodge School into the space but local people convinced the Council that they valued the Park as it is. Since then, the Friends of Victoria Park have made great

Saturday morning football in Victoria Park

strides in fulfilling the community side of the bargain: to really make sure that the Park gets used to its maximum potential as a recreation area. There are Larks in the Parks with story-telling, games and hands-on arts and crafts; 60 boys play football each Saturday morning; there are fun football and cricket events and the local nursery school brings children down to help with tree planting.

There is something of a tradition for Victoria Park to keep up. Would you believe that after the Crimean War there was a one-armed, one-legged cricket match here? I presume that some of the participants had lost a limb – or two – in the war and the other participants temporarily immobilised a limb – or two – to make the game fair. That is the spirit!

Friends of Victoria Park have been good about planting new trees. Tim Leicester is determined to have a tulip tree but has twice been given something else. There is a hope that wild cherry trees and two sweet chestnuts will provide future fruits and that two horsechestnuts will provide conkers. Someone planted a weeping willow for their mum, and someone transplanted a little hornbeam from their allotment. As well as the wild cherries, the Friends have planted ornamental cherries, *Prunus kanzan*, which have deep pink blossom in dense clusters, and bird cherry of which there are already some in the Park. The bird cherry has much bigger leaves than you would expect a cherry to have: as long as 10cm and 7cm wide, on grooved short red petioles and with sunken veins. Flowers are in pendulous buddleia-like sprays and fruits are black and spherical. I know all this because I did not recognise the tree and had to carefully note its characteristics and look it up. Another new ornamental cherry has been planted: a great white. Is it so called, I wonder, because as we stand under it looking up at its intense white blossom it is like being under the belly of a great white aquatic predator?

Victoria Park
in spring

When we say that the Friends have planted the trees, we should say that they have bought – or acquired – the trees, the Council contractors have dug holes for the trees and then the Friends, usually with the help of Muriel Green Nursery School children, have planted the trees. After that, a Friend of Victoria Park 'adopts' the tree: keeps an eye on it and meets any needs – like extra watering – when necessary.

So much for the new trees and the future, but already the Park is rich in mature trees. As we come from the top Verulam Road entrance we are under a London plane. Its leaves are such a bright green and it is such an airy tree that even in the evening there is no feeling of gloom under it. Next to it is an even more venerable plane. Its girth is nearly 4 metres (390cm, to be precise) and it is probably the age of the houses along the road. They were built in 1840.

There are attractive maples, some strikingly variegated green and cream. There is one on Verulam Road that catches the eye and Donato has captured in his photograph one bathed in a shaft of late evening sunshine.

There are loads of lime trees and they all have flowers sparking off in different directions. According to Alan Mitchell, this is distinctive of small-leafed limes, our native limes.

And we must not fail to mention a super oak on the Folly Lane side, or the wild meadow being 'cultivated' in the lower part of the Park. This is to encourage little animals, insects and wild flowers and herbs.

In the same spirit of biodiversity, when a substantial tree died, the Friends thought it would be good to leave it there for woodpeckers and beetles and agreed with the Council that this would be the right thing. The Friends had just planted some wild clematis to climb up it, blinked, and whoops! The tree was gone: the Council contractors had cut it down. The clematis has grown well and the Friends have extended the stump with a bit of trellis to amplify it.

This is altogether a lovely park, well cared for by everyone concerned, and ours to enjoy.

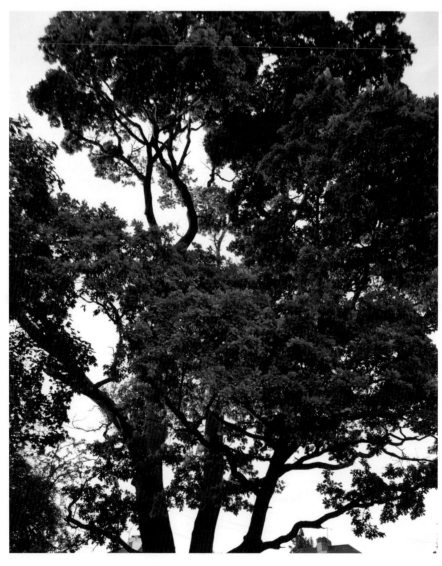

An oak in Victoria Park

THE REMARKABLE TREES OF ST ALBANS

Bernards Heath

There are several different parts to Bernards Heath, each an exceptional community resource. There are two fields where we can play wide games and youngsters and dogs can run about; there is wild parkland, some of it more wild than others, some of it more parkland than others; and there is woodland.

Upper Bernards Heath is a wide open space along Sandridge Road

The top field – or upper heath – is along Sandridge Road, lined with the alternating red and white cherry trees that commemorate the Second Battle of St Albans. Within the open space is a fenced and hedged playground with brightly coloured equipment for children to climb and swing on and slide down. The lower heath is adjacent to the upper heath down a short slope through a line of trees on the far side from Sandridge Road. We shall come to that later.

An exceptionally graceful maple at the corner between the upper heath and wild parkland

The trees along the town-side edge of the upper heath, between the asphalt path and the houses, are pleasant and spreading and there is a particularly attractive maple in the corner at the end of the path. It has wonderfully wide slender curving branches and tiny shrimp-like flower buds in April.

If we go through that corner of the upper heath we come out on to the end of Heath Farm Lane and across from it is part of the wild-parkland of Bernards Heath. There used to be a dairy farm here and most of this area was grazed until the 1930s. It is interesting to think that all that we can see and are about to see has grown up since then.

We cross Heath Farm Lane and take the left-hand path into the wild parkland area. At first we are within a belt of very tall ash and poplar trees (see Mrs Meakin's poplars in 'Our favourite trees'), and then come out into a magical space, mown but otherwise untamed. There are lovely hornbeams, a

Through a belt of very tall trees we come into a magical mown space

natural small leafed lime in the corner to the left, and a beech tree ahead on a path leading us away to the right. We follow that path by the beech into more wild and wonderful vegetation – lots of elders with their large umbrella-shaped white flowers in May and glossy sprays of purple-black berries in September – and then follow a path to the left that takes us out onto Harpenden Road.

My next-door neighbour in Walton Street, Ella Bevan, was born in 1904 and she told me that she could remember the cows lumbering across the road here to graze on the other side. We shall do as the cows used to do and cross the road – with care because drivers put their foot down to get up the hill and do not seem to notice that the road has levelled out and the extra acceleration is no longer required.

We are now on the west side of Harpenden Road in more formal parkland. To our left is a wonderfully wild wilderness – definitely worth a wander some other time – but we shall go straight ahead under the big maples and huge

A flowering maple in more formal parkland west of Harpenden Road

Blossom on the gigantic bush outside Spinney Cottage

beech to a gigantic clump of what looks like blackthorn but is in fact a species of plum. It is a mass of white flowers in April and has sweet dark red fruits in September.

Spinney Cottage is behind the plum and we go right on the track outside the house, down into the woodland section of Bernards Heath.

We soon see the deep dips where bricks were extracted. Local people refer to the pits as 'the bumps' but they are more than that, a perfect natural playground for cyclists who love to speed down and up the long steep slopes under tall trees. Trees are most substantial along the left edge of this strip of woodland, but are all large enough for us to marvel at them being less than 80 years old.

Our path comes out onto Harpenden Road close to The Ancient Briton and we cross over onto the path opposite that takes us up the hill through a mirror image of the strip of woodland we have just left.

Towards the top of the path, we pass the Lombardy poplars at Heathlands School and come to the complex of Judo Club, Pioneer Club, old fire station and ambulance buildings. We go left behind them on to the lower heath, cross the space or skirt it, and aim for the path through the far line of trees.

At the top of this path between lower and upper heath, we come to a tree that is worthy of comment. It is a sizeable oak that Jennifer Faldon nominated

An oak between
the upper and
lower heaths. It is
older than any of
the other trees on
Bernards Heath

as her second favourite after the Abbey cedar. It is particularly significant
here because it is obviously considerably older and more substantial than the
others anywhere on Bernards Heath.

We have been within a stone's throw of the centre of town and yet in
open space, parkland, wilderness and woodland. St Albans is a remarkable
place.

Highfield Park

Highfield Park is where the former Hill End and Cell Barns hospitals were.
There are some magnificent trees here planted when the hospitals were
founded at the end of the last century, and the Highfield Park Trust has

Lovely mature trees in amongst the housing and here alongside the Trestle Arts Base

done an inspirational job in preserving the trees, creating a village green, commissioning works of art, providing recreational areas for picnics, football, cricket, boules (petanque), providing children's play equipment – and planting exciting new trees and creating a Tree Trail round them. It is all mapped and explained in an attractive leaflet available from the Trust offices within the Park at West Lodge.

We shall follow the Tree Trail and discover its interesting trees, but in amongst the housing there are also amazing trees. In 'Our favourite trees', we were introduced to the giant redwood in Russett Drive, and outside the Trestle Arts Base we can see a beautiful set of mature trees. As we walk through the streets of Highfield we can look out for more of them – and perhaps take a stroll up to the Hill End Garden of Rest between Hill End Lane and the Alban Way cycleway and footpath. The small cemetery is something of a wilderness but mature trees spread over the indistinct little grave stones in a sheltering way.

The Highfield Park Tree Trail is well marked from the start. Numbers in the discs relate to information on the Tree Trail leaflet

The Tree Trail itself starts from a path leading out of the car park behind the shops on Hill End Lane. Significant trees are marked by a distinctive disc with a number that relates to interesting snippets of information on the Tree Trail leaflet. I do not want to steal the Trail's thunder, but do look out for the wonderful old London plane and old robinia to the left of the path

A purple sycamore stands tall between a sweet chestnut and a cedar with the old robinia lurking behind

at the start of the Trail. Each has bark that is knobbed and humped and grooved to a ridiculous extent. Neither bothers much with a canopy, unlike the common lime and purple sycamore between them and the red horsechestnut and copper beech on the other side of the path.

The Trail takes us to the edge of an orchard and then, in case we slip through the orchard onto Hixberry Lane and then to The Plough at Tyttenhanger, it slides us sideways past a new holm oak and a European larch into an attractively wild part. There is a mown path for us to follow and it leads us to a big turkey oak, a giant redwood, a deodar and the Indian bean tree nominated as a favourite.

A red horsechestnut has interesting branching, and still a few leaves in late November

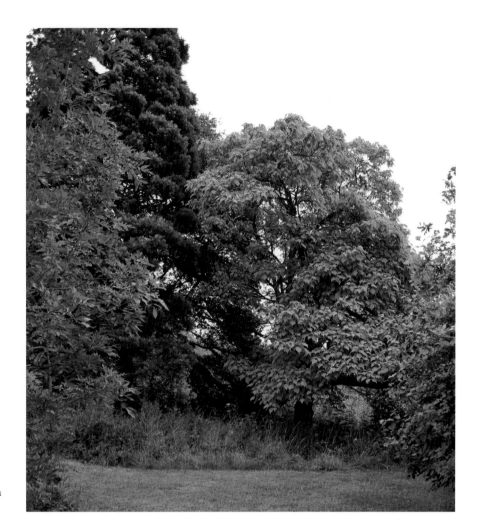

Mown paths lead us round the Tree Trial. Here we see a giant redwood and the Indian bean tree nominated as a favourite

We curve right round to another giant redwood and then two particularly attractive trees planted by the Trust: a dawn redwood and a swamp cypress. These trees each have dainty feathery leaves, the swamp cypress branches curling round like a dog trying to make itself comfortable in the blankets of its sleeping basket. The swamp cypress, the Trail leaflet confirms, can produce pneumophores, breathing roots, more handy in a swamp than at Highfield but who knows what climate change will throw at us.

Leaves of a wild service tree in the inner circle of the Village Green

The Trail then takes us across the bit the Trust is calling the Village Green. It has an inner circle of newly planted wild service trees, *Sorbus torminalis*. Rowans (mountain ash) are of the same genus but have a pinnate leaf, quite different from the lobed but entire leaf of the wild service. This is a native species but is not mentioned elsewhere in this book although most other native species are referred to many times over. The Trail leaflet calls it 'the forgotten tree of the English landscape' and it must have been more widespread than it is now because a drink, checkers, was commonly made from its fruit. The drink was so popular – or perhaps easy to make from ever-present trees – that many inns or pubs specialised in it and took their name from it. Most of the pubs called Chequers have a chess board on their pub sign but that comes from not knowing the origin of the name.

The outer circle of the Village Green is of hornbeams and in amongst them and outside them are self-seeded trees, oaks and other natives, and it is hoped that eventually we shall have native woodland surrounding the Green.

The Tree Trail takes us on along a line of oak trees planted by Groundwork Hertfordshire to commemorate the planting of 100,000 trees through the county following the great storm in 1987, and then takes us on across Hill End Lane into another great lobe of Highfield Park.

At first we go parallel and close to the road, past a lovely silver birch and on to where we cross Highfield Drive and go into Winchfield Wood with its mature oaks and some coppiced hornbeams. More native trees were planted here in 1997 to 1999 and it will be good to see how it all matures.

Apple trees in the old Cell Barnes Hospital orchard, trained along a fence line

THE REMARKABLE TREES OF ST ALBANS

After a good stretch, we cross Highfield Drive again and into what was the Cell Barnes orchard. The information board that tells us all about the orchard was not there when I passed recently but we can see apple trees trained along a fence line.

After the orchard there is a Norway spruce (our traditional Christmas tree), a pair of blue Atlas cedars and then a splendid beech tree by a maze with a winged totem at its centre.

Before we go forward to cross Highfield Lane back to the car park and reality, it is worth taking a moment to find the lines of ash and oak near the great beech. The lines mark old field boundaries and remind us how areas adjust and develop over the centuries according to our changing demands. Given that we have introduced extensive housing here, we have done well to retain attractive trees and plant many more.

St Albans churchyards

Abbey churchyard

St Albans most favourite tree, the cedar on the Sumpter-Yard side of the Abbey, and its young descendant on the north side; the wonderful beech tree at the northwest corner; and the delightful variegated maple at the east end have been spoken of in other chapters. There is also a handsome yew in the corner by the door into the south transept, and a glorious lime tree in the circle of grass at the west end.

Opposite:
Beech tree in the
northwest corner

Right: Lime tree
at the Abbey west
end

St Peters churchyard

Cedar of Lebanon
and other trees
in St Peters
churchyard

St Peters churchyard is the lungs of St Albans – it keeps us all breathing in our busy city centre. It is at the top of our main street tucked behind a trafficky roundabout and is a haven of calm and refreshment.

St Peters church has been re-thinking the role of their churchyard and, at the festival of St Peter in 2010, partners in St Peters Churchyard Community Project outlined plans to foster biodiversity and create a place of beauty and possibility, a place of remembrance and reflection. That sounds like a place where each and every one of us can go to be revitalised – and be welcome.

Entering the churchyard from alongside the gardens of the war memorial, we come into an avenue of limes and yew trees. By going right, we pass a car park that has been well designed to allow grass in amongst little concrete squares: 'grasscrete'. It is surrounded by shrubs and trees.

On our left is a fig tree, drastically pruned in 2009 but showing good leaves in spring 2010. As we near the southeast corner of the church our eyes are drawn left to an ancient cedar of Lebanon that puts our own short precious lives into perspective.

The churchyard has many of those tall solemn conifers that look at first very much the same as each other, but it is worth looking again. The first tall conifer on the right is a Western red cedar or *Thuja plicata*. It is not a true cedar (genus *Cedrus*) so to avoid confusion scientists prefer not to use the common name. Look in summer for the tiny cones. Spindle-shaped and upright, they are only a centimetre high but there are usually masses of them and they are an attractive contrasting yellowy-green until they turn brown in late autumn. Try putting the leaves to your nose. Do you smell pineapple? The aroma is a distinguishing characteristic of *Thuja plicata*.

Tall thin conifers

Some of the conifers have a look of layers of candlewax dripping downwards. If they have grooved bluish chickpea-shaped beads on their leaves, they are Lawson cypresses.

The conifers at the end of the churchyard have much more swirly cheery foliage and some have abundant orange-pink flowers.

The Garden of Hope in St Peters churchyard

Paths cross at a horse-chestnut at the entrance of the Garden of Hope, named for the sentiment expressed on its stone sculpture: 'God is with us' we are told on one side, and 'There is Hope' on the other. There are plans for a mediaeval knott garden round the sculpture. Nathaniel Cotton's walnut (see 'Paul Arnold's trees planted for their historical connections') sways welcomingly above and beyond the sculpture. Remembrance services are held here and we see at the far end the small stones commemorating people whose ashes have been interred in the Garden. The low wall has been repaired and beds of herbs and vegetation low in height and in maintenance will be planted in the raised bits, and benches made and placed in the recesses. We can sponsor the benches. Leave a note at the office on the other side of the church (the north side, between the church and the octagon room), or speak to the vicar or churchwarden, perhaps at one of the church's delightful Wednesday lunchtime concerts.

Coming out of the Garden of Hope and turning left, the churchyard opens out for us. Set well back on the left is a tree with glossy deep-green leaves. It is a stupendous bay tree that mocks the clipped little ornamental lollypops outside restaurants. Go near and smell the leaves.

In front and beyond the bay is an area to be left to develop naturally, a

An aromatic bay tree in St Peters churchyard

place for meadow flowers and wildlife to thrive.

The rows of young cherry trees on either side of the path are pretty with pale pink blossom in the spring. The trees were planted and are maintained by the Clifton Road residents. Thank you: a gift to us all.

Young cherry trees in St Peters churchyard

The apple orchard to the right of the path was the inspiration of David Curry. 'You don't have orchards in churchyards,' someone said to David. 'You do in this one,' he replied. The trees are coming on nicely despite some careless strimming round their rabbit guards. The oak in the centre was planted for Gracie Lawrence who worked at Ryders Seeds. She ran St Peters church youth fellowship for 40 years.

Gracie Lawrence's oak in the centre of St Peters churchyard apple orchard

As we turn back towards the church and take the right-hand path on the north side of the church and octagon room, we come beneath my favourite ash trees, branches flinging themselves outwards and upwards, freely and joyously.

And then we meet the path that runs parallel to St Peters Street. Almost everyone walking to or from town in this direction cuts through the churchyard to be away from the roar and fumes of the road. The bench on the path usually has a mum or two with pram or buggy, or a shopper having a breather. On the left of the path after

St Peters churchyard provides a refreshing break from the traffic

the bench, the trees round the Garden of Rest make it a shady haven of peace. A coppiced hazel and great lime tree draw us on towards the lichgate and then we are back to limes and yews at the way out to the town – and another reality.

Avenue of limes and yews, St Peters

St Stephens churchyard

In 948, Abbot Ulsinus built a church on each of the main roads into the town. St Peters in the north, St Michaels in the north west and St Stephens in the south on the road in from London.

St Stephens is an exquisite little church, made to look small by the absolutely wonderful horsechestnut on its south side. Words cannot do justice to its calm soaring spreading magnificence. To stand under it and look up within it is to come close to that which is sublime.

St Michaels churchyard

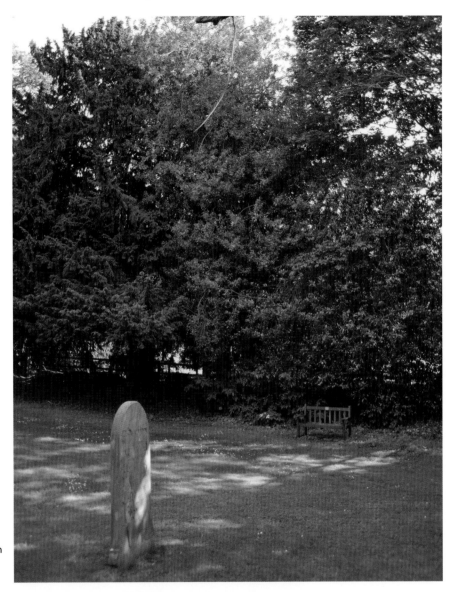

A holly has grown tall, into the sunlight

Opposite:
St Stephens horsechestnut

There is some interesting stuff in St Michaels churchyard. As we come in from the car park through the Ladies Gate – I love it – we are under a huge lime on our right and an English yew on our left. Beyond the yew is a holly tree of exceptional height. Slowly, slowly it has grown up and up and up into the sunshine. Notice how the leaves further up are not so barbed. Barbing takes energy that is not worth expending on leaves that are high enough to be out of the reach of browsing animals.

Looking towards the church we see clearly the difference between English and Irish yews: the Irish ones are darker and have upward-pointing branches like very tight candelabra and are the ones that lend themselves to topiary.

We turn along the path before the church, and the cedar of Lebanon ahead takes our focus. It is old and spreading and just as it should be.

Beyond the cedar on the path out towards Bluehouse Hill, our eyes are drawn to a massive red and grey trunk on the left of the path against the brick wall. This is a Western red cedar, *Thuja plicata*. It soars heavenward, as does the next tree to the right of the path. This is a coastal redwood, *Sequoia sempervirens*. It is a magnificent specimen of a beautiful tree. The foliage is distinctive and delicate: see how the leaves go in and out in waves like a necklace, and the branches have a jaunty lilt at their ends. In their native California the permanent sea mists keep the trees supplied with moisture and they grow to be the tallest trees on the globe. The *sempervirens* in their scientific name means 'always living' because it is unique amongst conifers in being able to regenerate itself after being cut down, rather like the hornbeams and hazels and other broadleaf trees after coppicing. They also sometimes take root after they have been blown down, and branches that fall off can start an independent life of their own.

Behind the coastal redwood is a collection of birch trees. They are not silver birches: their leaves are bigger and darker and their bark has a paper-thin white skin that peels and curls back. They are Himalayan birch trees, *Betula utilis*. Where there are scars on the trunk, there is a lovely rich red-brown colouring.

If we retrace our steps and follow the path under the great cedar – the paves of the path are grave stones – we see an interesting thing: on a plane tree, there is a branch from one stem to another that has completely fused to both. I have seen this fusing forced in mulberry trees in Agios Nicholios in Crete giving an arching cloister effect to the central reservation of a busy street, but it is not often we see it happening naturally. Here it looks as if the tree is offering to be a ladder for us.

Notice a sycamore tree that looks as if it has many stems. This is probably formed by growth from the base of a much older tree in the centre, now long gone.

A branch has fused to two stems

Irish yew and
cedar tree by the
gate to the village

With the church on our right now, we have three lovely cedars of different ages. The one nearest the gate is a particularly lovely shape. From St Michaels village it is a landmark, a life-affirming graceful culmination to one of the most attractive streets in St Albans, the prospect of which reconciles us to leaving our churchyard sanctuary.

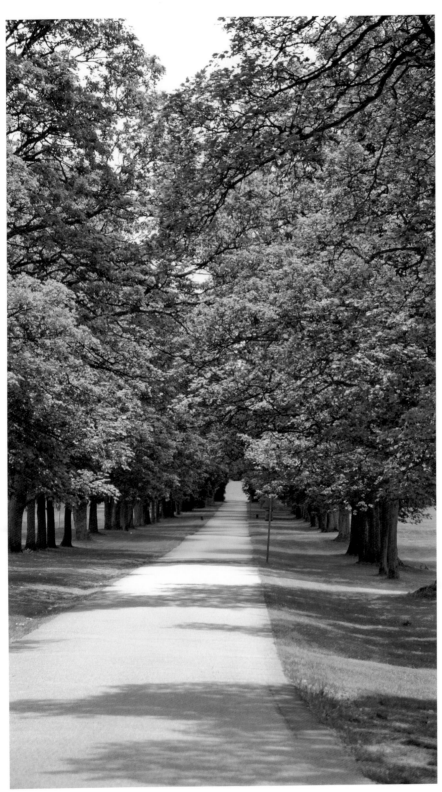

The drive into
Batchwood

CHAPTER
SIX

Batchwood

In Batchwood there is ancient woodland, post-war plantation, wonderfully varied mixed woodland and fine landscaped parkland – all on the same site within St Albans, and open to us all.

As we turn into Batchwood from Batchwood Drive we are in an avenue of maples of different ages interspersed with a few sycamores. The spread of the branches makes a rounded enfolding avenue, welcoming rather than imposing.

At the top of the drive we find ourselves under thrillingly tall trees. Most are limes but there is an occasional sweet chestnut and, if we look into the dense natural mixed woodland on the other side of the drive, we see a very tall ash tree disappearing into the sky. It is easy to locate because it is directly

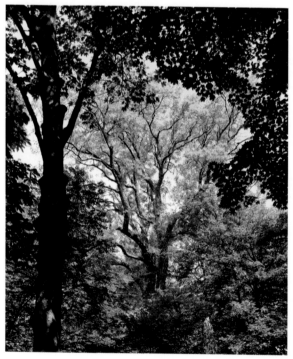

Old ash tree

behind the red-disk 'no entry' sign. Look well on this ash tree because it is very old and may not stay upright much longer. There are signs of burn damage on it but it is its age rather than injury that makes it vulnerable. When the ash comes down it will let the light through and different plants and little creatures will come in and thrive. Although I shall mourn the lovely tree, it would be appropriate if it fell in the Year of Biodiversity, 2010–2011.

We walk on and note Roma Mills' robinia on our right by the wall (see 'Paul Arnold's trees planted for their historical connections'). Ahead is the tulip tree planted to commemorate the last mayoralty of the City Council (see 'Trees with history'). You can imagine coming up the drive and seeing it a beacon of molten gold ahead.

As we pass Batchwood Hall, the house Lord Grimthorpe built for himself, and turn left alongside it, we find ourselves under a group of three wonderful beech trees close to our path – too close for the health of their roots, so savour the trees now. In April, their flowers spread a pink carpet across the grass under the horsechestnuts and sweet chestnut alongside.

A carpet of beech flowers from three beech trees spreads under the two horsechestnuts and a sweet chestnut alongside Batchwood Hall

The golf course is like traditional English parkland

As we reach the end of the Hall, an evergreen holly oak stands sentinel and we turn left under it, onto a path in front of the Hall.

What a wonderful open vista of landscaped parkland we have here. To the right a copper beech is set before the avenue of limes and horsechestnuts that line the drive down and away; still right, but on the near side of the fairway, a sweet chestnut stands proud of a whole collection of large trees running into the distance; in line across the front of the Hall are a spreading oak, Lord Grimthorp's plane, a red oak, an elegant silver birch and a huge holly; and to the left there are wide-branched conifers near, a towering sequoia further, and a bank of Scots pine, birch and beech beyond. There are wonderful contrasting textures and heights and blends of colours in the trees.

Mulberry tree

Near to hand, in the right-hand corner beyond the putting green, is a small building clad in slabs of elm. With most English elm trees gone, there will be few buildings in the future like this one.

At the end of the Hall, we come to a pair of fine oaks and turn right. The lumpy tree on our right is an ancient mulberry tree.

At the end of the line of rhododendrons on our left are groups of cedars and other specimen conifers and broadleafs. I especially like a silver birch that is more stocky than usual.

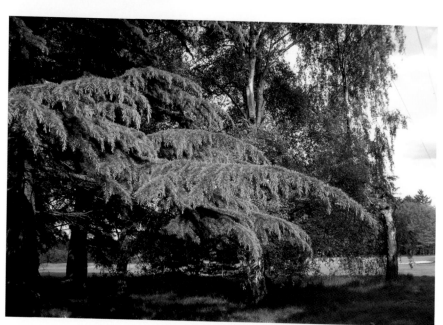
Group of specimen trees

The broad path into mixed woodland is one of my favourite paths anywhere. We shall come to good oaks on either side; an ash, a beech and a venerable horsechestnut in quick succession; paths and glades to the side, sunshine through trees to parkland, bluebells at our feet in spring and golden leaves in the autumn. And always we are aware of the awe-inspiring height of magnificent trees, majestic and calm with age.

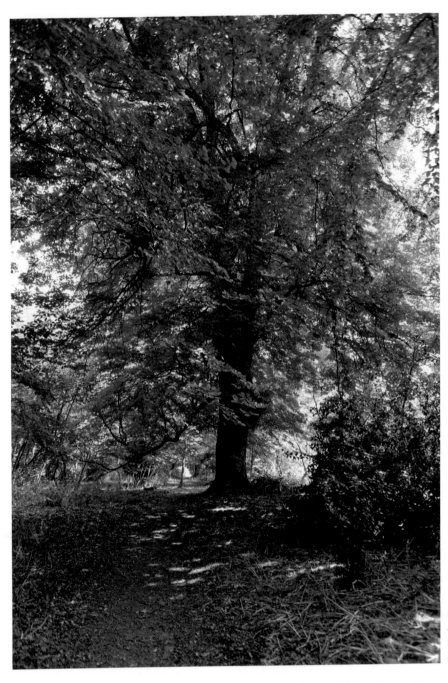

Horsechestnut
on one of the
best paths
anywhere

Our path was made for us by the Friends of Batchwood. The Council has responsibility for managing the whole site but it is ably assisted in looking after the woodland by the Friends of Batchwood.

In the picnic area on the left of the path is a willow, one of the varieties developed for the quick growth that makes it an ideal biofuel.

Miles Soppit of Friends of Batchwood shows us the type of willow grown for biofuel

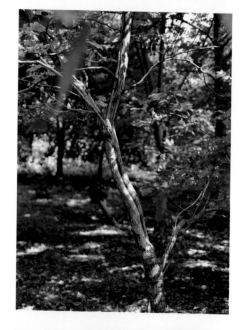

Squirrels have torn the bark from this young oak

An ash with a strip of its trunk peeled back

When grown specifically for biofuel, willows are coppiced and within three years will have grown multiple shoots ten feet tall and be ready to be coppiced again. Some shoots are retained for further propogation. They are cut into nine inch lengths and buried up to the last inch in soil. In three years they, too, will be ready for coppicing. The cut shoots are dried and burned, the energy used directly for heating or to generate electricity, in the process releasing only the gasses absorbed from the atmosphere during growth. Our own Rothamsted Research in Harpenden is working on developing the best willows for the job.

There is another willow behind the one at the entrance, and next to it we see an oak tree badly damaged by squirrels. It is heart breaking to find a strong sapling like this to be so injured after ten years of good growth. A humane squirrel trap is an attempt to keep the problem within limits.

Further along our path on the right is an ash tree that has a great strip of its trunk peeled back. This is like looking at a hedge-layer's work in magnification: see how the growth continues along the peel because the channels that carry sap up and down the tree are just under the surface of the bark.

We come to an opening on the right with a bench at the base of a huge oak tree. Look up at the oak and you will see that a good half of it has been torn away. This was done by the massive beech tree we see lying where it fell. In late autumn, the fruits of the fungus that did for the beech can be seen on its stump and all sorts of fungi along the log. We have lost beeches in Verulamium Park to the same fungus and there does not seem to be anything we can do to prevent it.

To see the coppicing down by the Friends of Batchwood and the hazel baskets they made to protect new growth, look out for a path on the left that has a particularly tall Scots pine at the far head of it. The baskets are on the right a short way up this path, some baskets of smaller stems, some using large and small stems. The Friends of Batchwood have done the kind of job that our ancestors would have done for millennia until the mid 20th century (see 'Tree Management').

You might notice an elm between the two kinds of baskets. If it is the right season, look for the typical round seeds of the elm and/or the lopsided leaves that feel rough and rustle with a paper-like sound when you feel them. If there are no leaves or fruit, look for a tree with a strong shoot growing alongside. The bark looks unaffected by Dutch elm disease and Paul Arnold has identified it as not an English elm but a Dutch elm which should be relatively resistant to the disease. Let us see whether it matures.

Much of the oak was torn away by the falling beech

Fungus on the beech stump

Fine-woven hazel baskets to protect new growth after coppicing

Dutch elm with a shoot adjacent

Creatures make use of tree stumps

By carrying on we come back to our original path and continue under soaring trees. The path ends in sycamore after sycamore in a lofty line. A six-foot stump beneath them is home for all sorts of creatures. We saw bees coming in and out of one hole, but presumably the holes have been made by different creatures for different purposes over time. It makes me think of apartments on four floors.

Out we come onto the drive. We could go straight over the asphalt and follow the path on the other side, but I suggest we go left and, as the drive curves left, cross it and go on to the path that has a yew tree hanging over it from the right. Note the yew hedge going off up the drive – I wonder if this yew escaped upwards from the hedge.

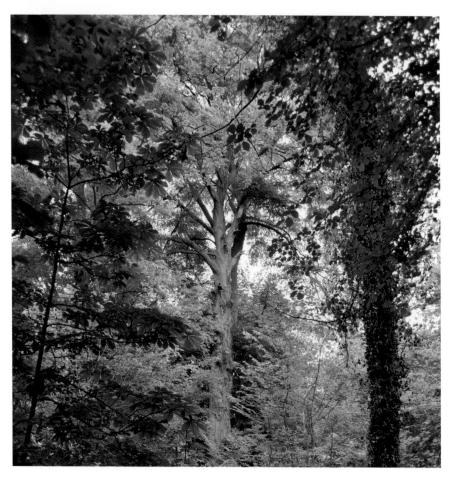

Beech that started life at the time of the Battle of Trafalgar

From the path, look up hill to the right and see through the trees an exceptionally beautiful beech tree. It has a girth of nearly 5 metres and must be more than 200 years old.

We come to a bench on the path (where the other path comes down). To the right are oak and ash trees that are particularly tall and straight, and a sweet chestnut so tall and straight that it does not have the usual distinctive twist to its bark.

Further along the path we come to deep buttresses at the base of an oak, a Turkey oak. The buttresses are a distinctive feature of Turkey oaks, as are their mossy-cupped acorns and the regular squared plates of the bark with redness deep in the grooves. Our tree is massive with a groove right up one side.

A turkey oak

We come
out alongside
an avenue of
maples adjacent
to the car park

Onwards and upwards we go passing new planting that is doing much better than in the glade at the bottom of the hill, and come out onto the edge of the golf course alongside the car park. The maple avenue here is a gem. Batchwood people call this 'Paul's leftovers' because Paul Arnold rescued the trees from the City Council's New Greens Nursery when it closed.

It is easier to get into the car park – or to continue on our Batchwood tour – from the other end of the avenue, so up it we go. The first trees are our native field maples with smaller leaves and seeds, then alternating red and green non-native maples. In the spring, we walk on a gold carpet of maple blossom.

It is decision time: we can either call it a day and quit now by curling back into the car park, or we can go on for a circuit round the northern woods.

Within the
avenue of maples

We in St Albans call this whole area 'Batchwood', but it is divided into two properties and so far we have been in the first property which consists of the golf course, the mixed woodland on either side of the drive up to the Golf and Tennis Centre, the Golf and Tennis Centre itself and Batchwood Hall. All this is now owned for us by St Albans District Council. Lord Grimthorpe left it to the City in his will. The second property is north of the first one on the other side of the strip of golf course behind Paul's leftovers, the tennis courts and the gym buildings. It is part of the Gorhambury estate.

If we decide to go on, we shall find that there are three distinct parts to the northern woods. You can see their different natures on Google Earth: a conifer plantation damaged by fire in the 1960s, the undamaged part of the conifer plantation, and ancient woodland. The parts are adjacent and edged along the northern boundary by what was once a laid hedge.

From the end of the maple avenue, we go to the right of the trees ahead, towards some high netting that protects the houses from flying golf balls. There is a pair of quirky conifers here. They have long tufty whiskers and

an elegant long thin green cone. They are Bhutan pines, *Pinus wallichiana*, a 5-needle pine. Look closely at the needle bases and you will see that the needles grow in groups of five.

Look back and see the typical shape – tall and narrow – of a lime tree at the start of the trees we are

Bhutan pine cone

passing, and compare it to the spreading lime ahead. Tree identification by overall shape is tricky.

We pass the spreading lime, go behind the netting and then, at the end of the netting, prepare to cross the fairway. We look left to be sure we are not

disturbing golfers and that we are in no danger of flying golf balls.

There is a clear path on the far side that takes us into the wood and then we turn left. We are now heading west and, from here to the west end of the wood, we have the first of the three distinct sections of the wood: the section of

Clear path into the northern woods

conifer plantation damaged by fire in the 1960s. At first we are surrounded mostly by conifers and then we find that there are different trees as nature has taken its course and filled in the spaces left by the fire. There is the inevitable sycamore, ash, and in some places silver birch. Towards the west edge of the wood, there are clearer patches created by the fire but for some reason not

The section of the plantation affected by fire: silver birch has come in to fill some of the spaces

Sometimes the spaces left by fire have not been filled by trees

filled by trees. The spaces make attractive sunny glades.

The way to stay oriented in this vast wood, I find, is to keep track of the edge so, at the southwest end of the wood, we turn right, heading north, with the wood on our right. This is a short stretch and we soon come to the northwest corner where we again turn right to keep the wood on our right and the boundary on the left. We are now heading east.

The girth
and shapes
of mediaeval
hornbeam boles
are thrilling

And here, all along the north edge of the wood, we have a feast of mediaeval hornbeams, distorted from being laid into a boundary hedge. The shapes, the girths, the twists and turns, the markings on the bark of these trees are amazing – and there are hundreds of them one after the other lining our path

Some stems are
horizontal from
having been laid

that might once have been an ancient lane, golden underfoot in the autumn, lined with leafy green light in the summer.

Lane along the
north edge of
the wood

Paul Arnold with his grandson enjoying squirrel telly in an ancient long-ago-laid hornbeam

Here is a lane to linger in, appreciating the weird wood shapes and textures, noting the different species: mostly hornbeam (see the distinctive vertical lines on its bark), occasionally ash (a pale bark with diamond patterned grooves) or hazel (ultra-smooth bark and almost-vertical, more-slender shoots) and even field maple (miniature maple leaves, crusty bark).

On our right, a good way along, the trees change from being conifer mixed with other species to being the second section of the wood: the conifer plantation undamaged by fire. Here we see the uniformity of the planting: strict row after row. First the area was clear felled and the timber sold for

The middle section of the wood: foresters planted the trees in strict rows and to a pattern

the reconstruction work so needed after the war. Grants and tax advantages were available to give land owners the incentive to provide the nation with what was required at the time – and foreseen to be required in decades to come. Paul Arnold worked in forestry in the early 1950s and tells how he was employed in just such planting – in Shenley, for example. The pattern is of seven trees repeated over and over again to the end of the row: oak, oak, pine, pine, beech, pine pine; each two paces apart along a straight row. On he went for a day's work of planting a thousand trees: oak, pace, pace, oak, pace, pace, pine, pace, pace... The Gorhambury estate must have employed just such a team to do just such a job. The idea was that, if the planting had been done evenly, there would be groups of four oaks and pairs of beech trees from adjacent rows. The plan was that the pine would be extracted earlier than the broadleafs leaving the standard oaks and beeches to grow to their maturity. But it did not work out like that. We can see that it is only on the edge that a few oaks survived. I can see no beech and oak as I peer into the depths of the plantation. The rows of pines are there but the oaks and beeches are missing from them. Also, twenty years on, the market had changed and the pine timber was not worth the extraction costs. So here we are with most of the pines that were originally planted.

More abruptly, we come to the third section of the wood: the ancient woodland, managed over the millennia since Neolithic times. Coppiced hornbeam is predominant, last coppiced decades ago so that the 'new' growth is way above our heads. As would have been the practice through

The third section of the wood is ancient woodland, mostly coppiced hornbeam and standard oaks

ancient times, standard oaks have been left to reach maturity in amongst the coppiced hornbeam. We can turn in amongst the trees if we keep an eye on our direction and know where the edge of the wood is, but it is a good idea to return to the north edge to keep oriented. We find the occasional coppiced ash, a tall cherry or two (one has three branches like the prongs of a trident), clumps of birches and, near the edge where the light is strong, all sorts of young growth.

As we traverse the northern edge of the wood, we come across a beam of wood set into the earth. This was put in place to stem the torrents of water that flow off the fields and down a watercourse through the woods. By the beam, there is a cherry tree of amazing girth and height. I was astounded to see that this ancient tree still bears fruit. We can continue skirting the woods or follow the watercourse back, taking the left-hand path when we come to a grassy triangle and going right when we come to the southern side.

Oak with burrs

Shortly before we come to the south side of the wood, we see an oak covered in huge burrs (encrustations) from top to toe. It looks obese. There is a species of oak called a burr oak, *Quercus macrocarpa*, a native of America, but its leaves are on petioles (stalks) of 3–5 cm, which is not the case for this oak.

The golf course can be seen on our left through the trees, all sorts of them flourishing in the light. I walked this way with Donato Cinicolo who took the photographs (the good ones) for this book, and we paused where there is a cherry log lying on the ground. The log is a whopper. It comes up to my thigh.

Donato Cinicolo on a whopping cherry log

Look out for a very odd ash tree: the top of it has died but is still hanging in there whilst new branches have forked out round it. The bark on the new branches is so different from that of the main stem that the branches look as if they are a different species of tree.

stem that the branches look as if they are a different species of tree.

As we come level with the central plantation, the path is somewhat wider and firmer than before and we are on what was made as a track along which to extract the timber. It has not yet been made use of.

When we are opposite the high netting where we know it is relatively safe to cross the golf course, we retrace our steps to the car park.

There is much more to discover in each part of Batchwood, in different seasons, at different times of day, in different weather, in ones different moods, with ever increasing awareness. We are fortunate to have such a source of refreshment in St Albans.

Track along which to extract the timber has not yet been used

Speaking of refreshment, we can usually get at least a cup of tea in the tennis centre. If the café upstairs above the gym is open, you will see from the window a glorious sycamore.

Sycamore across the fairway from the gym, dance studio and café

Harpenden and Rothamsted

Would it be going too far to say that it is the trees that make Harpenden so visually attractive? The town's architecture is pleasingly mellow but its trees are beautiful.

Ask Harpenden residents about their trees and the one that first comes to mind is almost invariably the ancient horsechestnut that is the first tree to come into leaf. It is on the corner of the High Street and Station Road and is included in 'Our favourite trees'. Then the 'baa lamb' trees are mentioned. This is a handsome group of trees opposite The Silver Cup on the main road in from St Albans. No one is sure why they are called this, and I suspect that both the name and its uncertain origin are part of the appeal.

Copper beech,
Harpenden Hall

The wonderful willows by the Lee in Batford get mentioned. They are chocolate-box perfect in their setting by the iron bridge. The huge poplars there and along the river are terrific: a little ford at the end of Crabtree Lane is as idyllic as it gets – and it is the surrounding trees that make it so.

What is surprising is that no one bothers to mention the superb copper beech at Harpenden Hall, Southdown Road. To anyone coming into Harpenden on St Albans Road, this is a most eye-catching tree, partly for its size, partly for its colour and partly for its position across the Common.

Residents seem also to take for granted the splendid row of green and copper beeches between Leyton Road (the one in front of the fire station by The Silver Cup) and St Albans Road, and do not bother to mention the array of horsechestnuts and medley of other broadleafs along the High Street in front of the shops.

My personal favourite is a tall tree in Leyton Green. It has a tapering shape and delightfully dainty foliage. It is a dawn redwood, *Metasequoia glyptostroboides*.

Dawn redwood in
Leyton Green

Another dainty tree of great beauty is a scarlet oak, *Quercus cochinnea*, planted by the Royal Agricultural Society to mark 150 years of experiments at Rothamsted. As you enter the research station at the main gate, the scarlet oak is on the corner in front of the pleasing red brick building on the right. Its leaves in autumn are bright scarlet and then gradually turn deep wine red, the lower branches holding onto their leaves, by then dark red-brown, well into the late autumn. Alan Mitchell describes the scarlet oak as 'wispy'. It will never reach the great stature we associate with mature English oaks but that teaches us to value the variety in tree form.

In Harpenden, ordinary places have lovely trees, some of them specimen trees. It is not uncommon, as we drive along the residential roads looking for an address, to find we are passing a white poplar or giant sequoia right on the verge; there is a splendid oak in the top corner of Lydekker car park off Sun Lane; there is a charming group of horsechestnuts in the green at the centre of Springfield Crescent.

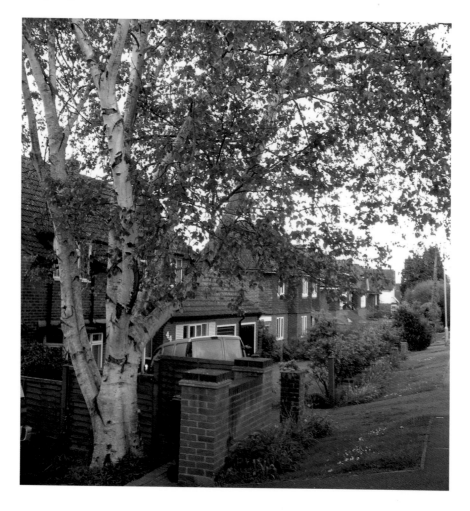

White poplar on a residential street

There is a horsechestnut on Grove Road that is a focus in the streetscape and, what I particularly like about it, is that kids climb it. The tree is on the edge of a purpose-built playground and it is as if the tree is an extension of the playground.

Robert Naylor-Stables

A host of tall conifers points heavenwards as we enter the Westfield Road cemetery, a pair of giant sequoias teaches us how insignificant we are, and the great copper beeches and other beautiful trees remind us how wonderful it is to be alive.

Hatching Green is on Redbourn Lane, not far from the intersection with St Albans Road. It is a proper green, a triangular open grassed area. At the top of it is a caricature of a beech tree; a caricature in that one of its branches strikes upwards and outwards at an acute angle, others at right angles, as beech branches do but usually less obviously. Once we have seen it, it helps us to recognise a beech tree in winter by its branch pattern. Next to it is a fountaining birch and then some horsechestnuts. Along the road edge are a hornbeam, a copper beech, a lime, a walnut and a mountain ash, each a first-rate example of its species.

If we cross the golf course on East Common from St Albans Road by way of Limbrick Road, we find we are passing through oak woods which, according to the information board on the Common by The Three Horseshoes, are self-seeded. The oak tree shapes are not what we expect: they are more twisting and spreading, branching lower than we are used to from hedgerow, garden or pastureland oaks.

And then we come to an amazing pair of three-needled pines. Their great trunks curve and coil outwards towards us and then up and up, great cones starting from the trunk itself, long clusters of needles forming their foliage. These are in the grounds of Limbrick Hall and behind them is what can only be called a crowd of Victorian trophy trees: a couple of giant sequoias, a true cedar almost as tall as the sequoias, and a throng of Western red cedars and Lawson cypresses. East Common ends Limbrick Road and, as we look along it to the right towards Grange Court Road, we see more and more colossal conifers. This is a remarkable corner of Harpenden.

Rothamsted Park

The avenue of limes is the first thing we encounter as we enter Rothamsted Park from the gates near the fire station in Leyton Road. The land slopes down and then up and away, heightening the effect of being led onwards.

There is a small formal park to our left, a picture of deep-pink blossom in spring, and there is parkland beyond on either side of the avenue.

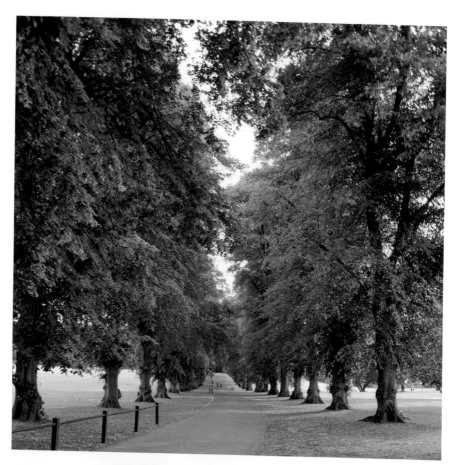

Avenue of limes, Rothamsted Park

A park within Rothamsted Park

At the top of the hill, we can take a path that forks to the right alongside the national willow collection. It is interesting to see the different textures, densities and heights of the growth, and to read the information board explaining how we are trying to find the best varieties for drought conditions, for wet conditions, for pest resistance and so on, and to find out about the wildlife the willows live with.

We are within the grounds of Rothamsted Research now and information boards tell us about the work being done and also provide maps showing rights of way and permissive paths that take us round the Manor.

Rothamsted Manor

There is a very pretty avenue of low-arching cherry trees taking us in towards Rothamsted Manor and, at the far side of the pond on the left by the low ornamental brick wall as we come on to the drive in front of the house, a great beast of an oak. It has a girth of 550cm – five and a half metres – and an amazingly textured trunk.

The two glossy leaved trees against the wall at either end of the house are *Magnolia grandiflora*, so named for the size of their heavily lemon-scented flowers, and the climbing plant close to the one on the right is a kiwi fruit.

Further along the drive is a ring of towering lime trees. There was probably a lime a generation older in the centre and these are shoots from it that have been allowed – encouraged perhaps – to grow to replace their progenitor now long gone.

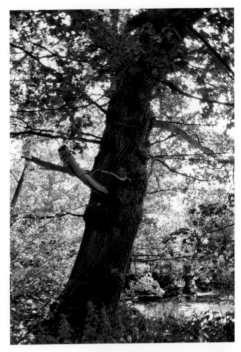

An old oak by the pond near the Manor house

A black walnut, *Juglans nigra*, has been planted close to the drive as it bends towards the house and, in amongst the bank of tall trees behind it, is an Asiatic elm, *Ulmus pumila*. It has not so far been infected with Dutch elm disease. It will never be a spectacular tree but it is interesting to see another species of elm.

Magnolia grandiflora flowers intermittently through all seasons

We are permitted to walk along the drive but, to go along the side of the Manor House, we have to wait until there is a Rothamsted Research open day, which I could not more highly recommend. There are graphic and tangible displays of fascinating information. Even from the drive we can see the magnificent pair of copper beech trees, one even older than the other and (on an open day), if we go across and behind them, we are in a space bounded on either side by the tallest imaginable trees. Our eyes are drawn to an extraordinary statue that is the reason for, and deliberate focal point of, our shaped space. It is a wild and wonderful sculpture, thrilling and frighteningly full of action

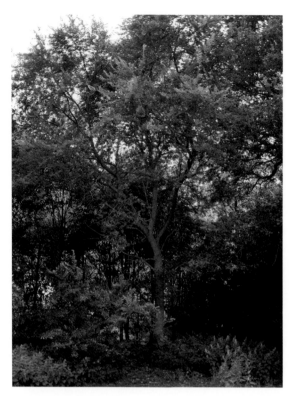

Asiatic elm

and energy. The woman being tied to the back of the frenzied bull is Dirce. She had tried to kill the mother of the two strong men, who are pinioning her down with ropes. We can see their names carved in Greek, Zethus and Amphion, and that of the sculptor carved in English, Charles Bennet Lawes-Wittewronge, one of the members of the family who owned the Rothamsted estate.

Behind the statue rise giant sequoias. Does their calm immobility enhance our awe?

The walk back from the sculpture towards the Manor is made superb by our glorious copper beech trees.

Returning to the drive and continuing on, we come to a row of venerable lime trees, hemlocks, yews, a coastal redwood and the giant sequoias that

Giant sequoias make a fitting backdrop to an extraordinary sculpture

back the sculpture. There are impressively tall trees along the path that takes us steadily round to the far side of the house.

Across to the west on the far side of the fields is Knott Wood which, despite having been clear felled in 1937, is designated ancient woodland. This is because there are unambiguous records of it having been managed woodland for 400 years. Oak and beech were planted in the 1940s and it is interesting to see how many more of them have survived than those planted in amongst the pines in Batchwood. There is a path along the edge of Knott Wood and between the path and the adjacent

Copper beech
at Rothamsted
Manor

field there is a line of ash trees. It is such a definite line that I thought they
had been deliberately planted as a hedge. A first! An ash hedge! But, no,
the trees are self seeded. Next time I passed I was amazed to see that the ash
trees had been laid. I should not have been surprised to find that it was the
photographer for this book, Donato Cinicolo, assisted by his wife Rosie, who
had laid them.

CHAPTER EIGHT

Villages, woodlands and the countryside

Wheathampstead

As we come down Brewhouse Hill into Wheathampstead, we see the soaring spire of St Helens church ahead backed by a distant bank of trees of every texture and shade. As we descend, the closer trees take the view and our eye is drawn to a golden robinia in a garden in the foreground on the right, and then to a great floppy walnut on the left with the zigzag brick-in-flint of the old school beyond it. And now we are abreast of St Helens: a cherry on the pavement, picturesque with blossom in the spring and with crimson leaves in the autumn; a tall larch, bright green in spring, dark green in summer, dripping in cones

Corsican pines
at the top of
Ash Grove in
Wheathampstead

all year; an even taller towering lime; and an over-arching magnificent wing nut, *Pterocarya fraxinifolia*. At first, I mistook the wing nut for a walnut because both have big rich-green compound leaves and early soon-shed male catkins, but there is no mistaking the female catkins of the wing nut. They are pendulous, pink and as long as an adult hand, elongating to twice that length and strung with circular winged green fruit in summer. After the wing nut are a couple of Irish yews and some Western

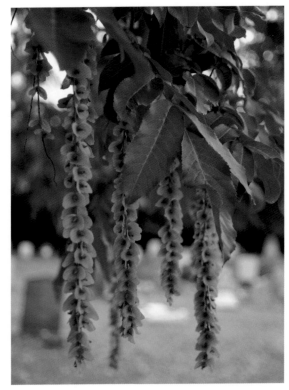

Caucasian wingnut

red cedars and then an Indian bean tree, which is one of a pair. Wow! What an entrance!

We might be tempted to turn in alongside the old school to have a closer look at St Helens. If so, we would be in Bury Green and we would immediately see at the top of the hill ahead a group of exceptionally large pine trees. These are Corsican pines and one of them has a girth of more than a metre. If we are tempted to take a closer look, our climb up the hill will be rewarded by the majesty of these conifers. If we follow their line and continue down Ash Grove, at the bottom of the hill we come to an ash tree that is pure joy to look at. While I watched, I saw tiny tits at the very tips of the twigs starting about

One of a pair of American Indian bean trees flanked by Irish yews in St Helens churchyard

Cedars in
Canons Field

and changing places with their mates, darting off as a pair of magpies jumped closer and closer, too heavy to get to them: but the tits took no chances. The tree has a lovely spreading shape from a stately stem.

We can curl round along Ash Grove until we find ourselves in Canons Field, an open recreation space, where there are lovely spreading cedars and a huge red oak right next to the children's play area. It has bracket fungus so we need to savour its grandeur while we can. See how its branches reach out and twist upwards. Find its small button-like acorns with their patterned cups. Note its large leaves and proper petioles.

A path leads us down into St Helens churchyard where there is another feast of trees.

Coming into Wheathampstead along the Marford Road are attractive old and young cherry trees and whitebeams. Along the river, are huge poplars and willows: everywhere trees adding to the beauty of the village of Wheathampstead.

Sandridge and Heartwood Forest

I love the tall Scots pine on Sandridge High Street. It is in the grounds of Lyndon House, very close to the road behind a curved flint wall and a hedge. The top of the tree seems particularly tall against the sky and has a graceful shape.

Heartwood Forest is the name the Woodland Trust has given to the vast area it is now responsible for in Sandridge. It is to be the largest new native forest in England. 600,000 trees will be planted and there will be wildflower meadows, orchards, vistas and rides.

Heartwood includes the ancient Langley Wood where St Albans people go to see bluebells in spring. It is a magical wood. Just thinking about being within it makes any tension roll from the shoulders. It has been managed in the past as a hornbeam-coppice and oak-standard wood and there are parts of it that have been coppiced more recently than others, encouraging biodiversity. Along the south-western side of Langley Wood there are some attractive old lime trees, but they do not quite compare with the venerable

Scots pine,
Sandridge

spreading small leafed limes in Well Wood, which is bit further up the main
path that comes up from the village and passes Langley Wood on the left and
then Well Wood on the right. If we know what we are looking for, the limes
can be seen as we approach Well Wood from Langley Wood. They are not of
the tall-thin variety but have round crowns. Even within the wood they are
not easy to get to because the undergrowth is dense and the paths within the
wood do not go particularly close to them. However, if we take the path that
skirts the wood on the Sandridge side, we can see them clearly.

The Woodland Trust is hoping that paths through these woods will develop naturally as we find our way through them. There is good access now and we can walk through any time, but it is worth attending the bluebell and summer festivals, planting trees and joining working parties in Heartwood. We can link up with super people in welcoming helpful volunteer groups, sign up for newsletters and make donations to help with the work that needs to be done. The obvious starting place is www.woodlandtrust.org.uk or call 0845 293 5706 for local organisers.

Bricket Wood

Bricket Wood Common is as ancient as woodland gets and has been designated a Site of Special Scientific Interest (SSSI). How dark and weird it seems as we turn into School Lane and find ourselves in a tunnel of trees with almost no undergrowth beneath them. Further on it opens out and, although the trees are still predominantly hornbeam, it seems lighter and there is more undergrowth. Further on there is a section that was clear-felled to re-create some of the heathland that was more extensive here a century ago when Commoners exercised their grazing rights. Trouble was taken to protect newts and other pond life but the contractors' equipment made deep ruts that filled with and held water, making the place a quagmire for ages. Silver birches have colonised some parts of the area, others have been kept clear as heathland, and there are

Hornbeam and standard oak at Bricket Wood Common

plans to bring back grazing. One of the reasons the site was given SSSI status was that wet acidic heathland, which is what we have here, is rare. The area has also been designated a High Biodiversity Area and St Albans District Council, the Countryside Management Service, DEFRA and Capel Manor College are all working together to undertake projects to optimise biodiversity. There are plans for more information boards, so watch this space.

Acidic wet heathland within Bricket Wood Common

The lessons of damage by heavy equipment in Bricket Wood Common were learned and, when it came to working in Blackgreen Wood, which is north of Bricket Wood Common off Lye Lane, horses were used to extract felled timber. The plan is to tackle a fifth of the wood each year for the next five years: coppicing and felling and undergrowth clearing. There is a lot of work to be done here, and the Council also has Nottlers Wood and Mutchetts Wood to look after.

Hanstead Wood in the grounds of the HSBC Training College is being capably looked after by the Friends of Hanstead Wood, and they have received a Green Pennant Award for the work they have been doing, planting native trees, putting up bird and bat boxes, creating a small delightful wildflower meadow and creating picnic facilities. Anyone can visit and be welcome. Turn into the training college (signed on Smug Oak Lane), turn into the car park, and you will see the entrance to Hanstead Wood. Within the wood was a tree nursery for the stately home that the college building used to be and there are lines of trees about a metre apart, tall and thin and straight, presumably planted as seedlings and never planted out. The specimen trees that *were* planted out in the parkland can be seen as we come into the site.

The Friends of Hanstead Wood meet to do what needs to be done on the second Saturday of the month and would welcome volunteers. They even have their own website: www.hansteadwood.co.uk.

London Colney

Willows, silver birches, a great horsechestnut and a neat rowan turn the space on either side of the High Street bridge over the Colne into an idyllic spot for picnickers, children fishing for water-life and imbibers at The Green Dragon. On one side, the silver birches make an inviting glade tempting us to a riverside walk. On the other side, a footbridge beckons us to the tree-lined lakes made from old gravel pits.

Trees make an idyll of the river bank by The Green Dragon

The Colney Fox has soaring broadleafs and conifers behind it and the High Street has lines of alternating maples and the odd lone pine to soften the scene and lift our eyes from the road.

And then there is Napsbury Park.

Napsbury Hospital was founded in 1898 and was an asylum for all but a few years of the whole of the 20th century and a military hospital in the First World War. William Golding designed the grounds and Napsbury is thought to be the only complete surviving instance of his many prestigious landscape designs. Golding's designs are informal and at Napsbury he took care to preserve existing trees, which accounts for the wonderfully mature native trees as well as a staggering collection of the specimen trees Victorians delighted in.

Broadleaf trees
behind The Colney
Fox

I thought I knew what to expect of Napsbury. Victorian rectors competed to have the best specimen trees and we have Hill End Hospital grounds and Cell Barnes so we know to expect cedars and sequoias and so on. But Napsbury has the real wow factor. Yes, right from our entrance, there are grand horsechestnuts, red ones in the central reservation, a good copper beech, a golden ash, cedars of Lebanon, deodar cedars, Atlantic cedars (blue and green). It is all magnificent and wonderful. What is exceptional is the scale of the planting. There are whole groups of magnificent trees.

As we go up a side road within the estate we see a whole line of Atlantic cedars stretching out into the countryside carrying our eyes to the water tower at Napsbury's sister asylum away over at Shenley. Beyond it is a shimmering great poplar backed by a line of Lombardy poplars and broadleafs and conifers away to a huge old comfortably spreading tree.

Closer in, across a lawn from the converted asylum buildings, is the hugest hornbeam I have ever seen, its branches dripping with its distinctive clusters of golden three-winged seeds. And what can that great spreading tree be? Amazingly, it is a wild cherry, its trunk the girth

Hornbeam seeds

An ancient cherry tree

of an old beech. Speaking of which, there are several of them – huge beings – and an ash, and a Lawson cypress or six.

Close to the water tower is a dawn redwood. It is darker green than the one in Harpenden's Leyton Green and probably twice its age. You should be lucky enough to see the cones. They are nearer spherical than cones usually are, a bit bigger than a hazel nut, not as big as a walnut, grooved horizontally, green in September, dangling on a stalk. Can you see the tiny pointed growths on the underside of some of the leaves at the base of the

Dawn redwood cones

leaflets? This is distinctive of the dawn redwood. They are leaf buds. See how floppy the growth is at the end of the branches and how much more strongly the leaves above twist and flare. As the autumn progresses the leaves will turn pink and then red and finally fall. Yes, it is a conifer, a deciduous conifer – as is the larch.

Further on, across a line of mature wild cherries and an asphalt path, is a tall turkey oak. See how narrow the leaves are and that they are each on a stalk, unlike our English oak, and the plates on its bark are as wide as my hand. Turkey oak acorns take two years to develop and our tree had few acorns in 2010, but I was able to find one or two, not completely formed but with the very distinctive cup covered in curls that curl upwards on the upside and downwards on the downside. A bracket fungus is evident at the base of the turkey oak, and part of its bark has been torn away. This latter wound is very sad, but it is nevertheless interesting to see the depth of the outer bark crust: it must be 12cm thick. Behind it is an English oak. It better beware the knopper gall wasp that will love it here with generation after generation of wasps alternating within their life cycles between the handy English and Turkey oaks.

Bracket fungus at the base of a turkey oak

On a happier note, also close to the turkey oak is a bird cherry, one of our undisputed 33 native trees. See its spherical black berries and buddleia-shaped blossom in spring.

Tucked behind a house at the edge of the parkland is a five-needle pine. It has whiskery needles and abundant cones narrow but longer than the length of my hand. They drip picturesque droplets of clear resin when they are green.

As we look through to the parkland we see spreading oaks and beech trees, glimpse a crimson king maple and note the spiky conifers.

Clear resin dripping down the cone of a five-needle pine

Along another drive there is a whole group of three-needle pines, Corsican pines I would say. Because they are so grouped they are spectacular: an array of silver-patterned trunks beneath, a riot of bristly foliage above. Behind is the

Corsican pines

kind of bank of trees we are more used to: soft blue-green birch, spreading brighter beech, pointed pines, feathery ash. Elsewhere there are masses of purple prunus, a rich burgundy in summer and glorious with blossom in spring.

Napsbury is an exceptionally lovely park to have within the District.

Redbourn

Avenue of limes across Redbourn Common

Coming towards Redbourn from St Albans we see a group of Lombardy poplars on the left, and then a group of huge glossy lively spreading poplars immediately before the filling station. Less than a hundred yards further on, at the roundabout entrance to the village itself, there are more poplars and willows. The village is at the confluence of the rivers Ver and Red, hence the water-loving poplars and willows.

Redbourn is on Watling Street, the Roman road straight as a die from Marble Arch to Holyhead. For millennia, travelers have paused here for refreshment and supplies. In the middle ages, pilgrims, tradesmen and craftsmen came to the priory; in the 18th century well-to-do families built substantial houses and planted prestigious trees; and trees in private gardens and public spaces have been planted and tended up to the present day. As I gaze out of the window while I am strengthening and lengthening my back during Pilates classes in the top-floor Guide room of the village hall, I see trees of every different hue and texture, shape and size.

There is a public garden through the great green double gates on the High Street. At first we are in a short avenue of English yew trees, some female with bright red fruits, some male without. Our heads are drawn back to follow upwards the height of a giant sequoia on the far side of the wall. There are lovely new trees in the garden and dark Irish yews. If we go through the arched gate and go left, we come out onto the Common. In the autumn there is a carpet of gold and deep red at our feet from the

New trees and yew trees

fallen leaves of a grove of mature maples, and ahead of us is wide open space with an avenue of limes stretching across the Common towards Church End. There is a cedar next to the old school away to our left (south) and beyond that a playground set about with cherry trees. By the river are mature weeping willows and poplars.

Trees round Redbourn Common

growth tendencies, its species, and the way it has been pollarded previously. In fact, once a tree has been pollarded, it needs to be pollarded again at the right time intervals. After regular pollarding the pollard heads become too weak to support a crown and the tree's life would be shortened if pollarding did not continue regularly.

Pollarding was not always done for the sole purpose of using the branch wood. For example, a tree might be pollarded to stand out as a boundary marker. This is unwise as, even after a single cutting, the multiple stems that grow after pollarding, if left to grow indefinitely, can become huge but not

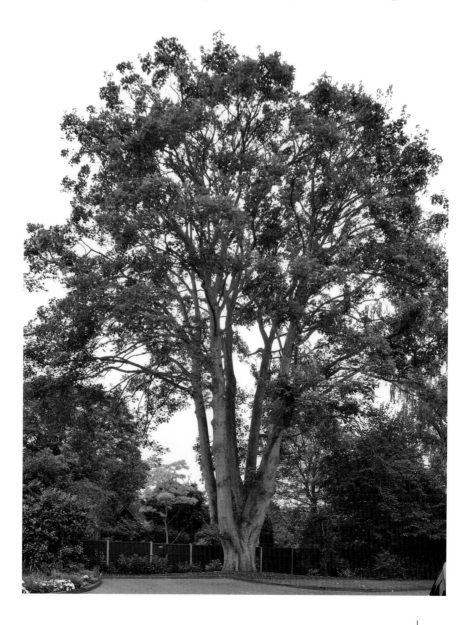

A wonderful pollarded sycamore

carry the foliage needed to sustain the tree as a whole, and the tree's life is shortened rather than lengthened. This is the case for an extraordinary sycamore within a private development in St Albans. It is a wonderfully venerable and substantial tree, but one-off pollarding, perhaps to mark a boundary, has reduced its capacity to support the crown it needs to sustain it comfortably.

Pollarding nowadays is spoken of by the Royal Horicultural Society as a method of pruning, useful if you need to limit the size of a tree that it is too near a house, has too wide a shade, or is on a street and would get in the way of streetlights, telegraph posts and wires. I think it is less confusing to speak of this as pruning because, if done well, the new growth continues through existing shoots. While we were photographing in Clarence Park, Donato Cinicolo showed me a copper beech in York Road that had recently been pruned well.

He pointed out that new growth was coming from shoots that had been left at the end of slender branches. It is difficult for a tree surgeon to reach those slender ends of the branches and it would be easier to cut the branch lower, but a good tree surgeon knows that, for mature trees like this one, it is best not to cut back below existing shoots that can carry on new growth.

A perfect pruning cut

The new growth after coppicing or pollarding is juvenile growth from under the bark rather than from within the tree. The managers of the trees in Hatfield Park claim that some of their oaks are more than 900 years old and put their longevity down to their pollarding.

One more thing: after standard oaks were felled, a single shoot of new growth from the stool would be selected and all other shoots cut back. The next standard would therefore come from the bole and root system of the original tree rather from a seeded sapling.

So we need not panic as some of us do when trees are being cut back. When Paul Arnold was working for the City Parks Department he was responsible for pollarding in Salisbury Avenue, St Albans. When he came back to the work after a lunch break he found a huge notice on the fence 'Council vandals'. He had meetings with the residents and explained that it was analogous to a hair cut or trimming our nails, but we cannot help but think of it as having

Location location

A second lesson is: we have to be careful how we muck about with where trees are.

An illustration of this is a study of the purple emperor butterfly. Like the purple hairstreak, the emperor lives in oak trees. It is to be found in the topmost branches. The male purple emperor butterfly comes down from the top canopy to drink the mineral-rich juices of dung or carrion and the female, after mating, lays her eggs on goat willow leaves, *Salix atrocinerea*, also known as 'sallow'. Goat willow is a shrubby tree found in woods and heaths and marshland or by ponds. The implication is that it is all very well planting our beautiful oaks in towns but we need to keep the ones near pasture, near woodland and near water, where purple emperor butterflies can find the other material they need to carry on the generations.

We can now add a third lesson: wildlife has complicated multi-dependencies, many of which we cannot yet know let alone understand, so that we had better be careful what we get rid of.

Good guys, bad guys

Advantage is not all on the side of the creatures that live off the oaks. Birds and small mammals, particularly, are useful to oaks. Jays carry acorns far and wide and hide them in just the right way for later germination. 'It has been observed' (just imagine the project) that a single jay can squirrel away 5,000 acorns in a ten-week period (Miles, 2006).

Who mentioned squirrels!

Now, grey squirrels really are a menace to oak trees. We saw in Batchwood the damage they can do. Does it add insult to the injury to know that tearing the bark in this way is a form of male squirrel display?

Lammas growth

Oaks have a specific ability to produce a second set of foliage in midsummer. It is bright green or reddish, which contrasts strongly with the existing matured dark green foliage. It happens around the beginning of August and, 1 August being Lammas Day in the church calendar, the new growth is known as Lammas growth.

One theory is that the Lammas growth is a consequence of moth-larvae infestations that cause a loss of leaves – which goes to show how adaptable and successful the oak has been in dealing with threats and also illustrates the co-evolution of tree and insects.

Lammas growth

Another perspective is that Lammas growth may by a case of adding more manufacturing capacity when energy allows in late summer. In general, in temperate regions with seasons like ours, trees get all their leaves out and up manufacturing nutrients as early as possible after the risk of frost. That is the way to take maximum advantage of the sunshine required for photosynthesis before sap must be withdrawn so that it does not freeze in the cold winter.

Whatever the trigger for the Lammas growth, it is a manifestation of adaptation to native conditions by a native tree, confirming our need to foster our precious native species: they are the ones that can hang on in there when the going is tough.

Altogether

Altogether, considering the inter-dependency of species and the effect of factors we might not dream of, we need to think twice before interfering with an environment that has reached a balance over a very long time.

Horsechestnut leaf-miner damage

Moving on from oak trees, no one can have failed to notice that the leaves of our horsechestnuts are turning brown long before autumn. This is because leaf miner moths come out of the ground round the base of the tree, climb up the trunk and lay their eggs on the leaves. The eggs hatch and the grub mines its way through the leaf

Leaf-miner moth grubs are attacking our horsechestnuts

munching on its nutrients and depriving the tree of proteins. It is said not to be life-threatening but it does weaken the tree.

You may have seen BBC footage in January 2010 of the efforts to protect the horsechestnut trees in the magnificent avenue across Boxmoor, Hemel Hempstead. Rather than attacking the moth, the experts helped the tree to survive the invasion by injecting nutrients under pressure into the soil around the tree.

There is a suggestion that the red horsechestnut might be resistant to the leaf miner moth. The red horsechestnut (*Aesculus x carnea*) is a cross between the North American red buckeye (*Aesculus pavia*) and the common horsechestnut (*Aesculus hippocastanum*). The red horsechestnut is smaller overall and has smaller leaves, which are often a bit puckered or twisted – and it has pink flowers. They are quite a popular hybrid and you may know of one. You can play a part in research to defend our horsechestnuts by keeping an eye open for red horsechestnuts and reporting to St Albans District Council Tree Warden Scheme on the extent to which they are being invaded by leaf miner moth.

Trees and the future

The Tree Strategy and Policy for St Albans was written within in the context of the Council's vision

> to preserve and enhance the distinctive character of St Albans city and District, making it an outstanding place to live, work and enjoy.

Many things make St Albans and St Albans District an outstanding place to live, work and enjoy – and the trees are one of them. I find I am not the only member of the community who thinks so. At two meetings I attended in the week of writing this, I was struck by how big an issue trees are for us: at a St Albans Civic Society meeting on the 'Past present and future of the Abbey Theatre', substantial time was spent on the trees that will be lost when the adjacent swimming pool is built; and at a talk on 'English Heritage and Verulamium Park', the loss of trees and concern for their replacement was the topic most passionately discussed.

Policy 1 of the Trees and Woodlands five-year plan is to 'ensure that the tree population continues to be developed and expanded with new planting where appropriate'.

Policy 2 emphasises the value of planting native species to maximise habitats for wildlife.

Policy 3 is a commitment to promote community understanding and ownership of our trees.

You will know from what I have written throughout this book that I support all of the above policies and want us to help the Council to fulfill the aims that the policies imply.

In these times of austerity, it is going to be difficult for the Council to fulfill the aim stated in the Tree Strategy:

> Many of our most notable tree-lined streets have tree populations that are over-mature.

> ...new trees should be introduced between the mature trees to ensure that there will be continuous tree cover in future years.

...the massive contribution that large trees make to the character of the environment must be maintained and safeguarded and be supported by new planting of similar species [forest type species]

The council will place a priority on the replacement of ageing street tree populations...planting large growing trees where appropriate.

This all adds up to a burden on resources to acquire the trees, to plant them and to look after them.

How can we help?

As individuals

Lots of individuals and groups are planting new trees and looking after them:

The Friends of Batchwood, the Friends of Victoria Park, the Friends of Hanstead Wood, the Friends of St Peters, and the Hertfordshire Orchard Initiative, for example, are doing sterling work. The Friends of Verulamium are desperate to unblock whatever it is that is holding up the planting of trees to replace the two hundred trees – yes, 200 – they state in their newsletter that the Park has lost.

Private individuals are doing their bit by planting trees in their gardens. Elaine and Roger Tate, for example, wanted a shelter belt between their home and the M1 motorway and, with the help of the Countryside Management Service, the Forestry Commission, the Woodland Trust St Albans Support Group, their friends and their own hard work, have managed to plant and will look after 850 trees.

We need to keep up the good work but also recognise that we can do something more.

This is where the Tree Sponsorship Scheme and the Tree Warden Scheme come in.

The Tree Sponsorship Scheme – planting new trees

It all started when the magnificent lime tree avenue in St Peters Street became of such an age that it was decided that the trees had to go. The original avenue of limes made the town centre truly beautiful in summer.

St Peters Street, St Albans, a century ago: 'One of the loveliest boulevards in Europe'

Elsie Toms tells us that St Peters Street was referred to as 'one of the loveliest boulevards in Europe', and that the St Peters Street lime trees were planted in 1881 at the expense of a private citizen, Mr H. Gotto (Toms, 1962).

But vwoop! They were all cut down and dug out.

It was Eric Roberts, then chairman of the Civic Society, who proposed a scheme of sponsorship to offset the huge expenditure required to replace all the trees. Eric had seen such a scheme work well in Folkestone.

The idea was that we could sponsor a tree by making a set financial contribution and the Council would commit to acquire the tree, plant it maintain it, and even replace the tree if required.

St Peters Street now

The Scheme was amazingly successful with many individuals, groups, schools, businesses and organisations contributing to it. All but one of the trees in our wonderful avenue of plane trees in St Peters Street was given under the Tree Sponsorship Scheme. If it had not been for the Scheme, St Peters Street – and St Albans – would be a very different place.

It had been foreseen that people would want to dedicate the tree in some way. Rather than commemorative plaques, a Tree Book of Remembrance was created and, for each tree, there is a page of commemoration with a beautiful hand-painted illustration of the tree – or some leaves and fruit of the tree – together with the dedication message written in perfect calligraphy. The illustrations and calligraphy were done by Linda Williams.

Councillor Bill Morris was just one of the other people who worked to see the limes replaced. 'Trees are the living furniture of our streets' is the dedication he gave to the tree that he sponsored.

St. Albans and District
Tree Book of Remembrance

Sponsored by St. Albans Civic Society
as part of a partnership with
St. Albans City and District Council.

Calligraphy and Illustration by Linda Williams.
Book made by I.R. Dorset of 'By George' 1999.

The title page of
the Tree Book of
Remembrance

Some trees commemorate a new birth or a person's life, some an event, a personal or family celebration, an idea or a thought or a success. Many commemorated the new millennium.

The range of tree species planted is impressive: beech, copper beech, silver birch, larch, oak, sweet gum (liquidambar), snowy mespil (no, I don't know it either), wild cherry, field maple, hawthorn, Crimean lime, flowering crab [apple], golden hornet, white mulberry, walnut and London plane.

As well as the city centre, sponsored trees were planted in Ragged Hall Lane, Netherway, Alpin Close, Forefield, Ramsey Close, Woodland Drive, Hatfield Road, Hamilton Road, Marquis Lane, Rothamstead Park, Clarence Park and Verulamium Park.

The dedications are inspirational and we can read them for ourselves if we ask at reception in the Council offices to see the Tree Book of Remembrance. Here are some of the dedications:

No said the bird, for the leaves were full of children hidden excitedly containing laughter

With gratitude for 21 years as Cathedral Organist and 40 years in St Albans

Happy years living in St Albans

'A fool sees not the same tree that a wise man sees,' Wm Blake

In celebration of Friendship and Goodwill – deep roots and many branches

For the Pleasure of Future Generations

To maintain a green heart in our City

For tomorrow

A record of gratitude for our Civic Heritage

As a living symbol of the role of Soroptimist International as a global voice for women

For a green St Albans. To recall the success of the 'Save Gombards Yew Group' and the help of Diane Fear

Rainbows Brownies and Guides: Future citizens of St Albans

To capture the beauty of Autumn

For the privilege of being mayor. 'The leaves of the tree are for the healing of the nations' Revelations 22:2.

For a green St.Albans

To recall the success of the 'Save the Gombards Yews Group' and the help given by Diane Fear.

London Plane
St. Peter's Street
2001

A St Peters Street plane 'For a green St Albans. To recall the success of the 'Save Gombards Yew Group' and the help of Diane Fear'

In 1999, a tree could be sponsored for £50, or more depending on the species of tree. This is much less than it costs the Council to acquire, plant and maintain the tree but it is at least a contribution towards the cost. The Tree Sponsorship Scheme gave us the avenue of planes in the main street of our city and many more trees along our streets and in our parks.

What of it now?

The St Albans Civic Society has a fund set aside to produce the pages of the Tree Book of Remembrance but it has not been called on for some years. At the time of writing, I have been told that there will be a staff meeting to discuss the Scheme.

Victoria Street used to be an avenue too. Would its restoration be too ambitious an aim for the revival of the Tree Sponsorship Scheme?

How Victoria
Street used to be

The Tree Warden Scheme – looking after trees

Tree wardens are a national force of local champions and a key part of the Tree Council's community action programme which gives people who feel that trees matter an opportunity to:

- champion their local trees and woods;
- plant and care for trees by watering new planting and replacing tree ties;
- carry out woodland management;
- set up tree nurseries using seed collected locally;
- survey local trees;
- provide early warning of threats, disease, decay and vandalism;
- involve their neighbours in tree projects;
- get together with like-minded people for training and field trips;
- spearhead Tree Council initiatives.

If you would like to join the St Albans District Council voluntary tree warden scheme, contact David Curry at the Council; treewardens@stalbans.gov.uk.

Together we can ensure that we pass on to future generations trees as remarkable as those that we inherited.